321 DOWN STREET

KEVEN CARD

321 DOWN STREET

For questions, media requests or bulk orders - Contact Us:
info@johnmichaelsjourney.com

ISBN: 0996268014

ISBN-13: 978-0-9962680-1-1

DEDICATION

Firstly, I want to thank my Lord and Savior for the grace He's gifted to an undeserving man, me. For directing my steps, which has led me to an amazing life and now a life that includes my beautiful son John-Michael. He has guided me through this book to its proper completion.

I'd like to thank my gorgeous wife, Marianne, who has always been and remains my first cheerleader and best friend. Without her I could never be the man that God intended me to be.

A special thank you to my extremely talented daughter who helped shape this book and who had to put up with my insatiable desire for perfection.

And to my dear friend Catherine Kingsbury who was gracious enough to tell me the truth when it was so necessary to make this project the best it could be. I will forever remain in her debt! Please take a moment to check out her blog: http://livinglikekingsburys.com/

A special thanks to The Rise School of Houston. You all have touched our hearts so deeply I can't find adequate words to express our thanks to you. Your love and support have meant the world to us as we've worked through John-Michael's challenges. Your dedication to the kids and to the Down syndrome community is unmatched. We love you all!

We also want to give a special thank you to Jan Stailey, Karen Dunlap and Cara Crafton. Each of you will always hold a very special place in the Card family and we just want to say… We love you all.

CHAPTER ONE

Bacon

Sara stared out the window in awe. The branches of the trees in the backyard swayed back and forth in the light breeze, the sun's rays piercing through the leaves causing shadows to dance across the wilted grass. Sara practically floated around the kitchen in her excitement which filled the room along with the smell of the sizzling bacon she was cooking. After years of being married, Sara knew exactly how to rouse her husband from sleep, and she knew that the aroma would eventually coax him out of bed. Elated, she let out a girlish laugh. *Today is going to be perfect,* she thought.

Sizzling and crackling sounds from the frying bacon echoed from the kitchen. She was certain that last pop would have woke him up but she didn't care because she was having too much fun. She let her hand rest on her pregnant belly, patting it affectionately. "I hope you like it out here," she murmured to herself and as if on cue, she felt a tiny flutter in her stomach. Being pregnant was unlike any other chapter of her life, she had never felt more purposeful. She felt like a mess of contradictions. Completely afraid and simultaneously stronger than ever. Powerful, yet unattractive but her mother-in-law had assured her that it was all just the hormones. It didn't stop her from feeling like a thanksgiving turkey, although she did appreciate everyone's attempt at making her feel better.

It wasn't long before Jacob's head peeked around the corner, sleepy eyed and resembling more of a toddler than a grown man. His golden hair was creased in the middle, pointing up on one side and flattened on the other. He flashed a smile at her, "What's all this?"

She chuckled, "You have some serious bed head Mr. Michaels."

Without a word he came up behind her, wrapping his arms around her waist and placing his hands on her stomach. "Should you really be standing up for such a long time, Mrs. Michaels?"

"I'm fine Jacob," she replied. "Besides the doctor said walking is healthy for me and the baby, so standing shouldn't hurt." She laughed patting his cheek playfully. He left a butterfly kiss where her fingers brushed against his lips.

"Well, if physical activity is helpful…" Her grin gave way to a full smile as she reached back to swat him. After a short pause he continued, "Seriously, do you know what would make this day better?"

She raised her eyebrow, expecting him to say something suggestive (which was typical of him). He spun her around in his arms so that she was facing him, her belly protruded slightly between them making him hold her awkwardly but he went on pretending she didn't notice. "I was just going to say, what would make this day better…" he trailed off looking deeply into her eyes. "is finding out we're having a boy today."

She let out a bark of laughter "Really, that's not where I thought you were going with that."

He pushed out his lower lip, furrowing his brows in mock offense. "Excuse me? What did you think I was going to say?"

She responded by stretching up on her toes to meet his eyes, trapping his face in her hands. They were an ocean that had seen its share of storms. Sometimes even she was surprised they had made it this far. Many people had their doubts about them, including their own families and now her heart swelled with gratefulness. Few men rose to the occasion the way that her husband did. After a long moment she pressed her lips to his. "I have severe morning breath," he said sympathetically in between kisses. Without another word she kissed him again.

"I'll be right back," he whispered with a smirk, kissing her hand like a prince might kiss a princess. After several minutes, he returned with a freshly bloomed red rose from their garden. He pressed himself as close to her as her body would allow, sticking the rose behind her ear and tilting her chin up for another kiss to which she happily obliged. She could taste the mint of their toothpaste on his lips and she smiled.

From behind them resounded a startling *pop*. They turned to see the splattering grease hit the burner, an angry flame was consuming the best part of their breakfast. In one motion, Jacob stepped protectively around Sara grabbing the lid to the pan using it as a kind of shield until he could get closer to the hot pan. With a loud *clang* he half-placed, half-tossed the lid over the pan and turned off the burner. He turned back to Sara. Seeing the fear and embarrassment in her eyes he said, "We should really get someone to look at this defective stove. I mean, spontaneous combustion should be covered in the warranty, right?"

She offered a small smile but she couldn't believe she'd left the stove on. Still, she was abundantly grateful for Jacob's light hearted response. She had dated few people before Jacob but all of them were hyper critical of her. She had thought that it was normal because that was how her family had been but when she had met Jacob he'd flipped her world upside down.

"You're amazing, y'know that?" She said burying her face into his chest. "How did I come to deserve such a great guy?"

Jacob let out a throaty laugh. "You're hilarious! You have it backwards. I don't know how I ever convinced you to fall in love with me but I hope I get to prove to you every day of our lives that *I'm* the lucky one."

She shook her head in disagreement but she didn't protest. She sighed happily into him as the light from the sun warmed their faces.

They found their usual rhythm in the kitchen. Jacob set the table while she plated their food. They danced around each other as they moved back and forth from the kitchen to the dining table, stealing kisses as they went.

"What time is the appointment?" He asked, mouth full of bacon (clearly, they had waited too long to eat).

"Ten-thirty" she answered, picking nervously at her food. Her former excitement had morphed into a sea of nerves swelling in her stomach. Doctors had always made Sara a little uneasy. The quiet waiting rooms and permeating smell of antiseptic tended to make her stomach flip.

"Great! That gives me time to go into work" Jacob started to say when Sara spoke up anxiously.

"Do you *absolutely* have to go into work today? Because, I kind of want you here with me." It was less of a question and more of a plea. The look in her eyes was enough to stop Jacob in his tracks and without any hesitation he agreed. She reached across the table and locked her fingers with his, gazing into his eyes and smiled at him in appreciation.

The joy of their morning juxtaposed with nervous anticipation continued on the drive to the doctor's office. Jacob looked over at Sara who was looking out the passenger window, wringing her hands in her seat. "It feels a little bit like Christmas, doesn't it?", he asked.

"Like we're about to open a gift we've waited for all year? Yeah…" She took a deep breath. She'd secretly hoped that they had done all they could to prepare a great beginning for their baby's life. She caressed her stomach in wonder. A small miracle was happening inside of her. Seemingly sensing her uneasiness, the little one wiggled slightly in her belly as if to say: *Don't worry, everything is going to be just fine.*

Without realizing it, they had both retreated into their own private thoughts, allowing a deep silence to spread in the absence of their words. The thought hung on her lips until she couldn't bear it anymore. Breaking the silence she asked: "What do you think it is?"

"It's a boy," Jacob said confidently, flashing a smug grin at her.

She rolled her eyes, "You're only saying that because you want it to be a boy."

"No, seriously. My grandma always said that if a woman's belly was round like a ball, it's a boy. If it's oval shaped, then it's a girl," Jacob said quickly in defense, glancing at her and then back at the road. "What?" he said shrugging his shoulders "It's true! The woman was irritatingly right about everything."

"So you've been reduced to old wives tales?" She chuckled.

"Let me guess, you think it's a girl?" he teased. She shrugged before responding cheekily, "Of course. I'll even bet you on it. But I want it in writing because if my memory serves me correctly you already owe me quite a few things."

"Deal. Back rub this afternoon. You can pick the place." He smirked, shaking her hand. Before releasing her, he lightly brushed a kissed across her knuckles "I love you."

She blushed, "I love you, too. Okay, let's do this."

CHAPTER TWO

4D

Sara surveyed the waiting room. Across from her was a slightly older couple sitting with a young woman who was obviously pregnant. The couple must have been ten years their senior but they held hands like they were newlyweds. They repeatedly whispered to each other while looking lovingly at their companion's round stomach.

"How far along are you?" Sara asked the younger woman.

"Nineteen weeks," She smiled sheepishly, tucking a blonde hair behind her ear. She was vibrant, the glow of pregnancy painted her cheeks a vibrant pastel pink.

"She's our surrogate," the older woman sitting next to her explained. Sara could see that the woman's expression was grateful with a slight hint of sadness. Just as she was about to curiously pepper her with questions, a heavy set black woman with a deep southern accent came to the door and called her name.

She and Jacob followed the nurse to an exam room which had peach walls and deep green floors. Though they had obviously tried to make the room feel more welcoming, the ever present smell of antiseptic was beginning to rattle Sara's nerves.

"Am I going to be sitting?" Sara asked the nurse, clearly confused by the position of the examination table.

"Oh no, Honey, we'll let you lay down once we get you on the table," she replied emphasizing her vowels with a southern drawl. "Doctor Earhart had an emergency today, so Doctor Osborn will be filling in, alright? Now, just hop on up there and the doctor will be in shortly."

Sara nodded as the nurse walked out the door. She looked at Jacob mildly concerned about her doctor not being there. Jacob rubbed gentle circles on the back of her hand with his thumb, which he hadn't let go of since the parking lot. She wondered if he could feel the anxiety that tying her in knots. "It'll be okay, it's just an ultrasound" Jacob whispered to her.

When the door opened again a very short and petite woman with dark, shoulder length hair wearing blue scrubs came in. She was closely followed by a beautiful young woman with tan skin and green eyes who barely looked up from behind her glasses. She sat directly in front of the computer screens that were lined up one by one filling the length of the small desk. "Good morning. I'm Doctor Osborn, I'll be filling in for Dr. Earhart today. This is Monica and she'll be assisting me today." Monica gave a quick, businesslike nod of her head.

"Are you ready to see your baby?" Doctor Osborn asked cheerfully. Sara was drawn in by her infectious smile and her calming presence.

"Yes, we are!" Sara said, excitedly looking at Jacob with raised eyebrows. His reflection mirrored hers because they had both assumed Doctor Osborn would be a man. Without missing a beat she added, "Can you tell us the sex of the baby today? We weren't able to find out during the last ultrasound."

"How far along are you?" she asked.

"Eighteen weeks" Sara replied.

Smiling even brighter Doctor Osborn said, "It shouldn't be a problem. Let me lower the table and we'll get started, okay?" she lowered the table until Sara laid comfortably back before lifting her blouse to expose her pregnant belly. The doctor seamlessly continued her routine, pulling out a tube of transmission gel and holding it over her belly button.

"This might be a little cold, okay?" The doctor

warned.

Sara nodded.

She held the tube just below her belly button, squeezing the tube until there was a small pool of blue gel. No matter how many times she tried to anticipate the feeling of the freezing liquid, it still came as a shock and her body shivered involuntarily. The cold seemed to reach around before shooting straight up her spine. She shuddered in response.

"You alright?" she asked.

"Oh yeah, I'm okay. Just cold." Sara replied excitedly looking at the gel.

The doctor took the eye of the ultrasound machine which looked like a worn stick of deodorant tethered to a long wire and used it to begin smearing the gel around. Within seconds black and white images began to appear on the monitor hanging on the wall.

Suddenly the familiar shape of a human head filled the screen. Sara smiled to herself, her heart swelling with an unknown emotion. It felt like love but was somehow stronger. She motioned for Jacob to stand next to her, wanting to indulge in the experience together. He gently slipped his hand into hers lifting it to his lips, his eyes glued to the screen.

The bet they'd made earlier still fresh in their minds, Sara and Jacob watched the screen like hawks for any indication of the sex of their baby. Acting as if the fate of the world depended on it (at least, his world did). Jacob whispered, "Bat and ball or dress up and tea."

"What're you talking about?" Sara whispered back.

"Well, this will determine whether or not I'll be teaching my son to hit a ball with a bat, or if I'll be forced to have tea parties with my daughter and fifty of her closest stuffed animals." His words were all for show because secretly he didn't care either way except for the bet he'd made with Sara.

Sara didn't mind him reconnecting with his inner child at that particular moment because it helped take her mind off the cold gel and how time had seemed to slow to a crawl. With every second that ticked by their anticipation grew and Sara could hear her pulse through her body accelerating. Jacob nervously tapped his thumb on her hand until he finally broke the silence and was the first to call out "I found it!"

"Found what?" Sara asked, perplexed.

"You know…" he said before glancing downward, then back up at her. When Jacob realized he wasn't making his point, nodded his head towards the ultrasound. "Don't you see it?" After a moment of silence, Jacob moved to the monitor pointing out a small protrusion on the screen. "It's right here."

"Um, that's the umbilical cord," the doctor interrupted with a chuckle. Sara rolled her eyes, somewhat embarrassed. "Right now we can't see the sex. We'll see if we can get your baby to move slightly so we can identify its gender." The doctor moved the ultrasounds eye to reveal more detail, jiggling the device to try and encourage movement but the baby ignored her promptings. She tried several more times but she got the same results. Finally, she said: "We'll try again in a few minutes." Sara noticed that the doctor was imaging her baby's heart again, which visibly thumped away on the screen. "Is everything okay with the baby?" The doctor replied with what felt like a canned response "I'm just getting all the measurements." Her words hung heavily in the air. Noticing the odd silence the Doctor continued, "There's no problem." Sara looked over at Jacob with a look of confusion and slight concern. He squeezed her hand in reassurance, placing a kiss on her forehead. "Everything is going to be just fine" he whispered.

Sara let out a deep breath attempting to release her tension and refocused on the screen. The baby turned and put his hands up to his eyes and yawned. A smile spread across her face: "Did you see that?" She squeezed Jacob's hand.

"I saw it!" he replied grinning brightly.

The doctor seized the opportunity and re-calibrated the eye to determine their big question. "There we go, you're having a boy." Monica, who was doing some indeterminable task on the computers while watching the ultrasound, heard the doctor's determination and drew an arrow pointed at a turtle shaped blob on the screen then typed 'B O Y' next to it. To Jacob it was like an official seal declaring his victory.

Jacob puffed his chest out in pride, he was beaming with excitement. He put his arms in the air in mock victory and danced around in circles. He ended his victory dance when he bent down and kissed Sara. Sara's faced seemed to glow a little brighter. "We're having a boy" she said "I can't believe it. I don't even have any names picked out for a boy."

"Uh-huh," Jacob replied absently, engrossed in his own excitement.

Sara glanced up to the screen and watched as the doctor drew another arrow. This one not pointing at a turtle blob but what looked like a golf ball and was an obvious image of the baby's heart.

Jacob bent down and whispered in her ear, "I won!" His words distracted her.

"I guess I owe you a back rub." She said in a less than convincing attempt to seem excited.

"Yeah, I guess I get to rub your back this afternoon." He winked at her grinning smugly.

"But you won!" Sara laughed.

"I know" he said without elaborating. His body

language said it all: he was a man about to have a son. The testosterone levels in the room had been noticeably elevated, at least to Sara. "I think our pastor preached about giving being better than receiving. I'm just practicing what he preached."

"Is that so?" She laughed again at her husband's obvious pride.

Their banter was cut short by the doctor: "Now, we just need to do the amnio and we'll be all done."

"The amnio?" Sara asked unsure what the doctor was talking about.

"The amniocentesis is the test that checks for potential birth defects. It was ordered by the Doctor Earhart, he should've already discussed this with you."

"Oh, that's right, he did." She said to the doctor then leaned over to Jacob. "I'm so sorry I forgot to tell you. After my last ultrasound, the doctor said I have excess amniotic fluid or something. He said it's was likely nothing but he wanted to do an extra test to be certain and I agreed because... well, you know me."

"Yes, I do," Jacob replied frowning.

"I meant to tell you but I forgot... forgive me?" She said putting on her best adorable face.

Jacob sighed, "Yes, I forgive you."

He looked up at the doctor. "How does this amnio, whatever it's called, test work?"

"We're going to extract a small amount of amniotic fluid and then have it analyzed. It'll only take about five more minutes to do the procedure. It will help Dr. Earhart determine if your baby has any chromosomal birth defects."

"And if he does, then what?" Jacob pressed.

"If your baby does have a prenatal birth defect, then both of you can discuss your options with Doctor Earhart. However, if you all decide that having a baby with a chromosomal birth defect doesn't matter to you, then we could forego the procedure all together."

"Is there any harm in knowing?" Jacob asked.

"There's no harm in knowing what to expect..." Dr. Osborn said taking a long deep breath. She seemed to contemplate her next words carefully. "Your child is beautiful and I know he'll bring you more joy than you can even imagine right now."

Monica, the technician who sat at the computers became noticeably uncomfortable. She shifted nervously in her seat before she said "I'm going to wait outside."

"Okay, I'll call you back in a moment" the doctor nodded. Monica bowed her head as she hurriedly left the room.

Dr. Osborn turned her attention back to Sara, she said cautiously, "I'm not here to tell you what to do. However, unless there's a very compelling reason to know this information, I usually advise my patients not to have this procedure done. It can put you in a complicated position, especially when couples haven't discussed the issue ahead of time."

Complicated position? I wonder what's she's talking about? Sara wondered. "Well, Dr. Earhart wanted me to have this done and I've always trusted him. Is there some reason I shouldn't?" she asked.

"No, Doctor Earhart is a fine doctor. I was merely stating my personal opinion. It's up to both of you to decide what to do," she said but Jacob could sense her nervousness.

"Well, I trust Sara and she trusts her doctor..." Jacob trailed off glancing down at Sara. She raised her eyebrows at him in approval before he looked back up at the doctor "So, I guess if Dr. Earhart wants it done, then we'll go ahead and do the test."

The doctor called Monica back into the room before she pulled out a syringe with a rather long needle. Jacob cringed. Sara pulled him towards her locking eyes with him. She winced for just a moment from the stick. Jacob didn't break eye contact with her, hoping it would take Sara's mind off of the procedure.

He pushed his own feelings about what was happening to the back of his mind, not wanting to scare Sara with what he was thinking. He secretly hated the thought of that needle piercing her stomach. He started to think of the worst case scenario but stopped himself to avoid any involuntary expressions that might cause Sara to worry.

It ended as quickly as it began "Okay, we're all done." The doctor handed Sara some wet cloth wipes to wipe the blue gel from her belly. With a grimace, she tried to wipe her stomach clean. "Here's a DVD of your ultrasound and a picture for you to take home" Dr. Osborne said with an outstretched hand "I just want to say it again, you're going to have a beautiful baby! I'll be praying for him and you."

"Thank you?" Sara said in more a question than a reply. "Have a great day," she continued cheerfully before she looked down at the 4D image of their baby boy's face, inspecting it in disbelief of the results. "He's smiling!" She said to Jacob beaming. *This day couldn't get better*, Sara thought.

CHAPTER THREE

Exhilaration

The ride home felt more like floating on a cloud. Sara held the picture in her hand. Everything else in the world had faded away into that moment. Her eyes fixated on the image of his face "I still can't believe it," she breathed.

"What's that?" He looked over at her from the driver's seat with warmth in his eyes.

"That we're having a boy!" she said exasperatedly, as if he should have known what she was thinking. A smile broke out over his face and reached his eyes. The sun hit his face and painted it gold, highlighting his usually light blond hair with orange streaks.

"It hasn't hit me yet either. I mean, I'm going to be someone's dad but it just seems so surreal" he said shaking his head while stealing a look at her while she was lost in the photo of their baby growing inside her. "Think about this, I'm going to be able to tell people I'm having a son. This whole thing still feels like a dream to me. How about you?"

"Yeah, same here" she sighed in contentment.

Jacob tilted his head contemplatively before reaching over and pinching her arm. "Ouch!" she exclaimed looking surprised.

"Nope! Definitely not dreaming," he said sheepishly. "Sorry, I didn't mean to pinch you that hard, baby."

She remained silent, watching as guilt washed over him. She looked out the window to keep Jacob from seeing her face. She took a deep breath as she tried to hold back but the intensity of the moment was too great. She erupted into a fit of giggles, her face turning bright red.

Jacob raised one eyebrow, obviously confused, "Wait… are you laughing?"

After a second she finally spoke, her words broken up by chuckles. "You… you fell for your own trick!" She was smug about getting him back. Jacob had played this game before and for the first time he was on the receiving end. Realizing that he was the butt of the joke, he joined her fading laughter. "Good one, smarty pants."

"I want to celebrate!" Sara announced looking once again at the picture in her hands. "Let's go out tonight. You want to?"

"Absolutely, where do you want to go?" he asked, his face beamed as he took her hand in his. If this day was any more perfect, it would have been too good to be true. His heart leapt. *Was it possible to love life this much?* he wondered as he wanted for her response.

"I want steak." She looked over at him, even she was surprised by what she was asking for.

"What? Really? I mean that sounds good to me but are you sure that's what you want?" He eyed her suspiciously, caught off guard by her request. Sara rarely ate steak in the middle of the day because it always made her sleepy.

"Yeah, and even more strange, I want mine steak the way you eat yours, rare, cold in the middle" she said scowling and holding her hands up in the universal language of 'I don't know'. She bashfully added, "I know it's crazy. Hormones I guess."

Jacob just looked at her confused. When Sara ate steak she always wanted it cooked so well it bordered on being burnt "You're right. That is crazy. I suppose you're at the mercy of your cravings now, next thing we know you'll be ordering anchovies with your ice cream." Jacob said winking at her.

Sara rolled her eyes, laughing, "You think you're funny don't you?"

"I have my moments." He puffed up his chest, closing his eyes in mock protest. He peaked at her sideways through his long lashes.

Sara just laughed, affectionately placing a hand on his arm and on her belly.

"That's my boy!" Jacob said proudly smiling. "He's craving good old fashioned red meat, just like his daddy."

"I certainly hope so" she said blushing. Sara held up the picture again to take it all in and then turned to Jacob, getting lost in thought while she gazed at him. She imagined him holding their son for the first time, rocking him swaddled in a blanket with his finger lightly touching his chin so proud to be a dad.

Jacob looked over and caught her staring intently at him "Hey, stop undressing me with your eyes!" he said..

Sara smiled brightly, shaking her head and rolling her eyes "Whatever..." she said.

"Okay, I see how you are..." Jacob said feigning disappointment.

"Can we just go now? I'm starving..." Sara asked seriously detracting from his playing. She almost hesitated because they'd already agreed to go out for dinner. But her cravings were starting to manifest in physical ways. Her mouth was beginning to water and her stomach was growling loud enough for both of them to hear.

"Sure, I think we still have time to make lunch," Jacob said pulling his phone out to check the time. "You know me, I prefer lunch prices anyway."

"Here we go again," she said poking at him. She could recite his speech about how it was a waste of money to go to fancy restaurants that inflate their prices for dinner. It was something he reminded her about nearly every time they went out on the town. "It's highway robbery" he'd say.

Jacob was always good with managing his money. He sold real estate and in his early career there were a few times when they had to tighten their belts until he sold another house. Sara thought that it made him a bit of a penny pincher but she didn't mind. That's where he learned to save most of his money for the down times. Although, in recent years he'd been selling houses at a fairly steady pace and they could easily afford to celebrate, she didn't want to get him started. "Okay but I have to pee and I need you to hurry" she said to avoid the inevitable reminder.

"No worries babe. I'll have you there in no time" Jacob nodded.

CHAPTER FOUR

Dinner For Two

"Table for two?" asked a young, attractive hostess. She was soft spoken with jet black hair that faded into blond. She wore a white button down shirt and a black bow tie that looked a half size too big for her tiny frame. Sara immediately liked her demeanor.

"Yes please, and..." Jacob deliberated for a moment, glancing down at her name tag, "We're celebrating tonight. So if possible, Heather, could we get something with a little more privacy? Maybe a booth toward the back?"

Jacob fumbled with the twenty dollar bill he held in his hand and smiling he offered it to her. The young woman looked at him, then at his wife and without taking the money gave a small smile in return. "I'm sure we can find something suitable for you both," she said and after a brief pause, conversationally she added, "Do you know what you're having?"

Jacob grabbed Sara's hand and proudly said. "We just found out today as a matter of fact. We're having a boy."

In one fluid motion Heather smiled, looked down at the touchscreen pad, tapping it with her finger quickly before pulling out two menus. "Well, Congratulations! I can tell you both are going to be great parents" she smiled, pausing just long enough before she continued "Your table is ready now, please follow me."

She motioned for them to follow her into the large dining room area. They walked through a maze of diners and servers before making a quick turn into a section where one other couple was dining. She walked straight to the corner booth and motioned for them to have a seat.

"This is perfect Heather, thank you" Jacob said gratefully.

He reached for the menu holding out the tip he'd offered her earlier. With pure professionalism and amazing precision Heather took the tip while leaving the menu in Jacob's hand. She placed another menu in front of Sara and said "You're server will be with you shortly. In the meantime, would you like to look at our wine menu?"

"Thank you but I think we'll both be drinking milk

28

this evening," Jacob replied to Heather while remaining fixated on Sara. She blushed under his intense stare. Jacob was nothing if not passionate.

Sara looked up at Heather who smiled and nodded "milk it is" she said before retreating back to her post.

It had been a while since they'd been out, just to enjoy each other's company. The day's news was the perfect excuse to ignore all the emails, phone calls and pointless everyday demands life pressed on them. They chatted amiably about nothing and everything the way they did when they first met and for a moment, nothing and no one existed but the two of them and their baby boy. Eventually, the food came and went with various waiters and waitresses attending to their needs. Sara couldn't decide which was better, the food or the idyllic silence she shared with her husband. She could sense his anticipation and obvious pride. They were both captivated at the idea of being parents and having a son.

After dessert, Jacob paid the check and they headed home, the crisp air and the glow of the city lights added a picturesque background of an already amazing day. When they arrived, Jacob swooped around the car to open Sara's door. He lifted her by her hand and when she was standing, he said "I believe I owe you a back rub, Madam."

"Why, yes you do," she replied teasing him with a

heavy southern drawl.

"Well, then why don't you go up and get yourself comfortable and I'll be up shortly" Jacob said.

"Now, Honey, don't keep me waitin, you know how I hate that," she continued her southern theme.

"I certainly won't Ma'am, you have my word," Jacob vainly tried to play along but he'd never quite mastered southern accents. Jacob waited until she reached the top of the stairs before he went to his office, unlocked his file cabinet and pulled the drawer all the way out. In the back he pulled out a bottle and looked carefully at it. "Prenatal massage and body oil," he read aloud. "I hope this works as good as the lady at the vitamin store said it does."

He'd planned on surprising her with a massage two weeks ago when he bought it but he'd gotten distracted with work. Little did Sara know that him conceding the bet earlier in the day wasn't a coincidence but another plot of Jacob's to surprise her. He grabbed it and darted upstairs taking them two at a time. He slowed his pace just as he approached their bedroom door in the hopes of maintaining his cool. He pushed the door open and stopped, the sight of her took his breath away. She sat on the bed facing away from him, the white glow of the bedroom lights glistening off her. Her hair was draped over her shoulder to her front. The beautiful olive skin of her bare back tapered before it disappeared into the crumpled comforter "Wow! I wish I were an artist… because if I painted what I see right now, it would be a priceless masterpiece."

Sara could feel her face getting warm as she blushed but he couldn't see it "Oh really, you think a painting of a pregnant puffy woman would be worth something?"

"Yes," he said plainly. As much as she complained about being puffy and fat from the pregnancy, from where Jacob stood you couldn't tell she was carrying a child at all. What he saw was her raw beauty and nothing she said was going to dissuade him.

"I'm glad *you* think so."

"No more talking," he said as he pulled off his shirt and crawled up behind her lightly kissing the base of her neck. "I just want you to relax." He opened the lid to the massage oil and went to pour some in his hands but nothing came out. He tried again but again nothing.

"What's wrong?" Sara asked.

"I can't get the oil to come out…" he said as he examined the bottle. He twisted the lid off. "Are you serious?"

"What?" she said turning around to see what happened.

"They put one of those tamper proof lid things on a bottle of massage oil. What are they afraid of, someone might drink it?" the sarcasm was clear in his voice.

Sara tried to hold back to keep the mood in tact but she couldn't. She burst out with a bellowing laugh and a loud snort filled the room.

Jacob joined in her laughter, "What was that all about?"

"I don't know…" she took a deep breath, "It just came out." They both laughed uncontrollably. After several minutes she begged "Okay, okay please stop I can't… I can't breathe." She intentionally took a long deep breath to try to calm herself.

"Are you ready for your massage now?" Jacob said trying to rekindle the mood.

"I don't know, can you get the oil out?" she retorted as she burst into laughter again.

Jacob blushed in embarrassment, "Okay, you got me. That was a good one. That stung a little" he said extending his lower lip giving her his best puppy dog look.

"Okay, okay I'm done. I'm ready now. Massage away" Sara said.

Jacob massaged her back slowly and intently for a long time before he could convince her to lay down on her side. He worked his way down to her lower extremities and while working on her feet he heard the soft sound of her snore. "Sara?" he said quietly to be sure. When she didn't respond he knew that she was fast asleep. He pulled the comforter up over her shoulder kissing her lightly on the cheek. He wiped his hands with the shirt he had discarded earlier and crawled under the covers, snuggling right up behind her and drifted off to sleep with her in his arms.

CHAPTER FIVE

Unexpected

Sara liked to keep herself busy during the day while Jacob worked, so most days she found herself organizing and reorganizing the nursery. Today, she put her idle hands to work sorting the baby clothes by size, putting them away neatly in the drawers Jacob had just assembled a few hours earlier.

Her eyes lingered over the newborn clothes her mother had just bought, they seemed impossibly small in her hands. She couldn't help but imagine him. Would he have brown hair? Blue eyes? How much of him would look like her? The unexpected ring of her cell phone startled her out of her reverie.

"Hello?" She answered.

"Hello, this is Vanessa from Doctor Earhart's office. I'm calling for Sara Michaels?"

"This is she. How may I help you?" She wondered

what the doctor's office was calling for. They had just been in for a checkup not long ago. Her thoughts accelerated into benign questions. *Had something happened with the insurance?*

"Doctor Earhart wanted to schedule a time for you to come in to discuss the results of your amnio."

"Okay. When?"

"Well, he had a cancellation for this afternoon at four. Would you be able to come in then?"

"We just had that test done barely a week ago. Was there a problem?" Sara's increasing anxiety was becoming evident in her voice as her mind raced.

"Honestly, Mrs. Michaels, I don't know. I was just asked to call you to see if you could come in. The doctor can explain everything this afternoon. Can you make it in at four?"

"Of course." Sara said hesitantly, her words seeming to stick to the back of her throat. "Of course, we can be there."

"Okay, we'll see you here at four. Thank you." The call ended but she couldn't bring herself to take her eyes off of the screen of her cell phone. Sara couldn't shake the feeling of foreboding that was slowly growing in her chest. "Jacob!" She called out. "We have to go back to the doctor's office at four."

"Today?" He replied baffled as he poked his head into the nursery.

She was on the floor leaning against the crib, her

hand resting on her belly. Her mind was dizzy with possibilities. When Jacob's eyes met hers he instantly knew something wasn't right. "Yeah, the doctor wants to go over the results of that amnio test." Her words were short and disconnected.

For a moment Jacob said nothing, he just studied her face. Then finally, he said calculatedly, "Did they say why?"

"No. I asked but the receptionist said the doctor would explain everything when we came in."

"Well, I guess we'll find out then." Jacob said making a space for himself next to her on the floor. She flipped her hand over so that her palms faced up and instinctively he laced her fingers through his own.

Sara looked up at the wall clock and the time read 12:22. Then she glanced at Jacob disappointedly. "We only have to wait three and a half hours, no problem." There was no disguising her distress. Only thirty minutes had passed since the doctor's office had called and already she had played a thousand different horrifying scenarios in her mind.

"Don't do that." Jacob said pointing his finger at her.

"Do what?"

"Don't start over thinking this."

"I'm not."

"Yes you are. I can see it all over your face!"

36

Jacob had always been a gifted reader of body language. It was something he'd developed early on when he became a Realtor. After many years of negotiating deals with people, you learned a thing or two about the ones who were serious and the ones who were just blowing smoke. It made it nearly impossible for anyone to lie to him and she was no exception.

He knew Sara's general reaction to the unknown was to worry about what might happen and it would sometimes take her on very dark journeys into the worst possible scenarios. Jacob had noticed her emotions being more pronounced than usual ever since she became pregnant. In this case he knew it was her way of preparing for the worst because the world couldn't disappoint her if she had already determined it was awful. It was just her way of coping with unknowns.

"Try not to worry. I'm sure it's nothing."

"What if...?" she started to say.

"Oh no, no you don't!" Jacob interrupted her pulling her into his arms. Tears pooled in her eyes and gently glided down her cheek until they were caught by Jacob's shirt. He squeezed her tighter attempting to comfort her but he knew that the only way to put those fears to rest was getting answers from the doctor.

They sat together for what seemed like nearly an

hour but when Jacob looked up at the clock it was
only 12:47. It was clear that time would fail to help
him in preventing Sara from worrying but maybe
sleep would. Jacob started to caress her hair unsure
who was more comforted by the act, him or her.

"Thank you" Sara said.

"For what?"

"For being here with me."

"I wouldn't want to be anywhere else" Jacob said
firmly.

"You always make me feel better."

It wasn't long before she had nestled comfortably
in his arms. She started to twitch softly, a clear sign
she'd drifted off to sleep. He glanced up at the clock.

It was 1:57.

"Getting closer." He mumbled.

He sat staring at the wall, his mind now wandering
into his own dark place. He shook his head as a flood
of horrific thoughts burst into his mind. "Stop that!"
he commanded himself, but the wheels of his mind
had already started turning. After what felt like an
epic battle with his own thoughts, the clock finally
reached the time he'd been anxiously waiting for:
Three o'clock.

He tapped Sara on the shoulder, "Honey, it's time
to get ready to go to the doctor's office."

She opened her eyes but was clearly groggy from
her nap. "Huh? Doctor?" She said confused.

"Remember, we're supposed to go see the doctor at four to discuss the test results."

"I thought I was dreaming." She said sadly.

"Nope, not a dream," he replied. "Not unless we're both having the same one." He tried to say it in a way that wouldn't expose his own apprehension.

She got up slowly, the dread of the impending afternoon meeting evident by the look on her face.

Jacob tried once again to counter her concerns. "Let's just hear what the doctor has to say before we go jumping to conclusions." His words were as much for him as for her.

The drive to the doctor's office was a stark contrast to their previous trip. It was somber and quiet, the hum of the tires over the road the only backdrop to the lack of conversation. Jacob parked in the first spot he saw, just then realizing he had been so consumed with his own thoughts that he didn't remember driving there at all.

The walk into the doctor's office was more like an out of body experience. They checked in at the desk and chose a seat in the corner of the room. Hand in hand they sat staring at the floor not even making an attempt at conversation.

"Sara Michaels!" The same nurse from their previous visit came through the door called out in her southern twang, scanning the room in search of movement. "Sara Michaels!" she called out again.

Sara and Jacob stood together both looking somewhat lost. Jacob raised a hand to identify them and started walking toward her. "Are you ready, honey?" she asked Sara, seeming to be in tune with her anxiety.

"Not really." She replied.

"Don't you be getting all upset now, Honey!" Sara looked up at her for any indication of what she might know but all she could see was her soft eyes and brilliant smile. "The Lord knows what He's doin'" was all she said as she escorted them down the hall.

An odd breeze blew down the hallway and a strange peace washed over Sara for just a moment then quickly faded as the nurse pointed them into the doctor's actual office. A cherry oak desk the central focus of the room along with a matching bookshelf filled with various medical journals and plastic anatomic models no doubt used for demonstrations.

The door opened and a man in a white lab coat walked in and immediately retreated behind the desk. "I'm Dr. Earhart" he said reaching out to shake Jacob's hand. "Sara, good to see you again. Thank you both for coming in on such short notice." Noticing the worry on both their faces he continued, "I don't want to cause any additional concerns so let me get right to the point. The amniocentesis that we performed during your last ultrasound indicated that the baby has Trisomy 21."

"Trisomy 21?" They repeated in unison.

"It's more commonly referred to as Down syndrome but in layman's terms it means that the baby's DNA carries an extra 21st chromosome. So instead of two it has three. Unfortunately that third chromosome 21 can be the cause of several potential problems."

"Okay?" Sara said not sure how to process what was being said.

He continued, "The baby will have developmental delays of one kind or another and almost certainly other, more serious complications as a result."

"What kind of complications will *he* have?" Sara asked exaggerating the baby's gender in recognition of the doctor's repeatedly odd "the baby" description.

"Well, the complications can range from constant ear infections to Leukemia and a host of others in between. Some of them develop serious heart conditions, epileptic type seizures are even a possibility. The truth is there are a whole host of potential complications that these children are susceptible to. I printed off some information about these potential complications from the Mayo clinic." He held the paper out toward them until Jacob finally reach up and took it.

"Is there a cure or some medical treatment or

something we can do?" Jacob asked searching for some solution he could grasp onto.

The doctor paused for a moment and took a deep breath "I understand that this is a shock but sadly, there's no cure for chromosomal birth defects." He waited for his words to settle before he continued "and I must warn you that life with a child who has one of these defects is almost always, extremely challenging. If you're not prepared for a life of complications and in some cases life ending complications, there are options."

"Options?" Jacob asked.

"It's early enough in the pregnancy that you could end it and try again in a few months." Dr. Earhart was clearly choosing his words very carefully.

End the pregnancy was all Sara heard. "What do you mean by end the pregnancy?" she said as if the words were spoken in a language she couldn't understand. The air suddenly thickened around her. Her breathing became rapid as she tried to rebel against the images that were being created under the weight of the Doctor's words. *It's not possible.* She thought to herself while visibly shaking her head. "No, you must be wrong! Your test was wrong!" She said forcibly. She turned to Jacob "We need to do another test because there's nothing wrong with my son" she demanded. Jacob was noticeably stunned by turn of the events and unable to react to Sara's outburst.

Recognizing Sara's struggle with the news, the doctor pushed a button on his desk phone and spoke into its speaker: "Can you send Nurse Hall in here immediately?"

Within a few seconds the nurse who had previously escorted them in knocked on the door and then slowly opened it. "Would you please take Mrs. Michaels to a room where she can lay down? And please stay with her until she settles a bit. Page me immediately if she gets more agitated."

"Yes, sir." She replied as if it were routine. She gently put her arm under Sara's and lifted, guiding her out of her chair and then out of the room. She walked with her down a short hallway into another room "Now Honey, what's got you all riled up?"

"My baby" was all she could say.

"Now don't you be worried about your baby. No matter what that doctor says, that baby is a gift sent straight from heaven and you just need to hold onto what God has given you." She leaned down to look Sara in the eye "The Lord knows what He's doin" she said again.

Sara nodded in agreement.

Jacob was still in the office and the doctor refocused and continued "As I was saying before, you have options."

Jacob paused for a long time before finally

responding "Yes."

"Here is some information about clinics that can assist you if you decide to end this pregnancy" he said it as if he'd just recommended a pediatrician, which Jacob found odd. "It's a relatively routine procedure, so your wife should be fine and at this stage in development the fetus can't feel anything. so you don't have to worry about hurting it" he said. Jacob felt the callous sting of his words pierce him deeply. "Look, I know this is a hard decision but let me add that many of my colleagues believe that it's more humane to end a pregnancy than to let a child suffer a life of unending medical and mental challenges." His words crashed over Jacob like a ten foot wave.

Jacob listened intently but couldn't speak, clearly overwhelmed by the gravity of the news. He just sat and nodded to acknowledge that he understood. The doctor went on: "As I said before if you aren't prepared for a lifetime of challenges then you should at least consider these options. Of course, that's a decision you and your wife will have to make. I wish you the best" he said plainly before he stood up and simply left the room.

CHAPTER SIX
Hazy Day

The ride home was a blur for them both. Each lost
in a sea of thoughts, the waves of despair
continuously crashed over them pulling them further
down. A raw sense of hopelessness seemed to reach
up from the depths to drag them under.

Silent tears streamed over the curvature of her
cheeks and dampened her blouse. She watched the
landscape blur past unable to fully come to grips
with the reality she now faced. Her heart ached, the
words "Down Syndrome" and potential
complications cut her heart like a knife.

The sense of desperation that Jacob felt was just as
consuming. Stealing a look at his wife, he felt the
pain that reverberated through her in his own
chest. Moisture filled his eyes before he looked away
to wipe them dry.

Jacob hadn't seen his wife in this much pain since the passing of her mother which had caught her by surprise and sent her into a tailspin of despair. She'd had trouble eating for weeks and wasn't able to sleep well for months. Now it looked like they were about to repeat the ugly, dark cycle. He could feel it. When her mother passed, Jacob had waited on her hand and foot. The only thing that really seemed to help her was getting reconnected with her childhood church. It was there that she'd rekindled an old high school friendship with her best friend Stacey.

Plus, the senior pastor had just passed away and his son had taken over; something about that had provided her with deep comfort. After that year, they made it a point to attend church as often as they could… at least for a while.

What would give her comfort now? Jacob thought bitterly. Sara led them in prayer every night over their baby as he formed in her womb. Sara had gotten Jacob to quote scriptures over her plump belly. Jacob felt betrayed. He began to think maybe all of this God stuff was just an illusion. They both stared blankly out the windshield. There were no words that could undo their new reality or diminish its pain. The feelings of excitement that had permeated the car only a few days before were now fully extinguished.

They walked through the door in silence. Sara

flicked on the hallway light and Jacob shut the door tightly behind them. There was only the dull thud of Sara's shoes against the wood floor and the sound of the car keys hitting the table in the entry way. He realized it was probably the only appropriate response to the devastation the day had brought on them. It was unfair. What had they done to deserve it?

Sara quietly walked upstairs to their bedroom with her head down to dismiss any idea Jacob might have had of trying to console her. She closed the door to ensure that he knew better than to follow. She wanted to be alone.

She slipped off her shoes and crawled under the covers of her bed. The pain overtook her right as she reached the bed. A gripping sadness burst in her chest and she clung to the edge of the bed like a life raft. The pain was so intense that she tried to call out for Jacob but all she could do was mouth his name. She quickly unbuckled the leather belt of her Topshop Maternity Jeans and tossed it but it did nothing to stop the twisting in her heart. She collapsed onto the bed stricken with fear she let out a loud, undignified sob that would have given a passerby chills.

Jacob heard her cry out and he sprinted up the stairs to the room, yelling, "Sara? Sara! What happened?" He burst through the door nearly taking it off its hinges. "Sara, what's wrong?"

Seeing her laying on the bed he went to her side and placed his hand in the small of her back leaning over her. She laid there staring out the window her silent tears now transformed into uncontrollable sobbing. "Baby, talk to me," he said.

"I don't...I don't understand." She said in between breaths. "It hurts so much...Why does it hurt so much?" Jacob attempted to soothe her by rubbing circles on her back. "I don't want to talk anymore..."

"That's okay, you don't have to..." he whispered to her, "just rest." Jacob was always good under pressure, putting his feelings on the back burner when he realized Sara needed him to be strong. He stroked her hair hoping it would calm her but after nearly thirty minutes he was starting to get frustrated.

"What do you want me to do?" He finally asked her.

"Nothing." She replied abruptly.

"C'mon you can't just lie here crying all day. Why don't we do something to get your mind off of this?" As soon as the words left his mouth he realized how cold they could be taken and tried to clarify. "I mean we could talk about it and maybe you'll feel better."

Again she replied in broken sentences through deep sobbing breaths "No....I just....want....to sleep."

"Do you want me to stay with you?"

She didn't offer any words this time she just shook her head no.

"That's fine I'll leave you alone." He said. He was a bit shocked and hurt by her response. She'd never asked him to leave before and he did everything he could not to be offended by her rejection but it stung. "Call me *if* you need me," he said sharply, obviously implying that she didn't need him before shutting the door a little too hard.

She could hear his frustration but in that moment she wasn't able to console him. Her own pain was more than she could bear, far worse than she ever imagined it could be. She was no longer just in pain, she was confused by the familiarity of grief that was engulfing her heart and taking over her emotions.

She closed her eyes weeping. Before long her exhausted crying gave way to sleep.

CHAPTER SEVEN

Lonliness

Jacob sat slouched, his body sank deep down in large cushion of the brownish-red leather chair facing his desk. With every sound that emanated from the interior of the house, he listened intently studying the still air, careful not to make any noise. He was desperately hoping that Sara would recognize the wound she'd left by her rejection and call for him.

He sat for hours, waiting at the ready to run to her side but the only sound he heard was the continuous beating of his heart in concert with the seconds of the clock on his desk which ticked in unison. With every heartbeat the darkness seemed to get thicker and the air heavier. "I don't understand" he whispered then quickly returned to complete silence still hoping to hear her voice.

His thoughts were focused on Sara. "What does

she want from me?"

3:21

The clock announced the late hour through its red digital numbers in the darkened room. Jacob's eyes grew heavier and heavier as the clock ticked ahead one 3:22. "Sara" he muttered as he unwillingly gave in allowing himself to drift off to sleep.

There she stood on the balcony of the hotel room. The cool night air lightly blowing against her dark brown hair, her dress swaying. Jacob marveled at her as the light reflected off her soft olive skin. She was half Caucasian, half Filipina what her mom called a "mestiza". But to him she was just beautiful.

It was easy for him to get lost in her beauty. The softness of her light brown eyes played off her olive skin and petite frame. He could recall for anyone the day they met. Every detail of that night etched into his memory forever. On command he could recite that night's events and how he'd stumbled over himself and his tongue as they shook hands for the very first time.

He was walking toward her when she turned and smiled at him, stopping him in his tracks. He smiled back at her as she turned and leaned against the balcony's rail and motioned him to come closer. He stepped out onto the balcony and reached out to wrap his arms around her. He wanted... *no, he needed* to tell her he loved her. It felt so strange the moment out of place but he continued toward her.

A sudden bright light blurred his vision.

The light blocked his vision of Sara. He finally opened his eyes, closed them and then opened them again shielding them with his hand. The sunlight had penetrated the barrier of the window shade rousing him from his dream.

Reality came into focus as he realized he was still in his office. Sara had never called for him. He was still exhausted. The brief sleep had done nothing to restore him at all. Anger welled up in him turning his face flush with frustration. He sat up in his chair now deliberating his current circumstances.

10:03

"I have to get outta here!" he said aloud grabbing his coat and sliding on his shoes.

The outside air was biting cold but he didn't notice because the heat of his anger seemed to chase away the cold air. Deep down he knew that Sara was hurting too but he felt pushed away and slightly betrayed. He was being suffocated by his feelings. He had to do something and a brisk walk in the cold air was as good as anything else.

"Why?" he demanded.

He glanced up long enough to see Linda jogging toward him. He only knew her by her first name and that she was the neighborhood 'I want to stay in shape so I'm going to jog everywhere to show off how fit I am' neighbor. She was noticeably attractive but everyone knew she also had a husband who was a competitive body builder. He was so muscular and fit, he moved more like a wall than a human being. Needless to say, even casual conversations with her was always kept to the bare minimum by nearly everyone.

Their three kids were rarely ever seen playing in the neighborhood but everyone knew they were heavily involved in sports. Every once in a while Jacob would see Linda taking the kids to some kind of martial arts training, each of them dressed accordingly.

As she neared to him he could hear music playing. A music player was strapped to her arm but she wasn't wearing any ear-wear. It was a duet of some kind and he could make out a couple of the lyrics *God blessed me broken, my eyes look to heaven.* She smiled as she passed by and he forced a smile in return.

"Hmm... God..." he said indignant. "What God?!" he asked as images of the doctor giving them their son's diagnosis and the words "Down syndrome" came to the forefront of his thoughts. "This is just God's cruel joke! I mean, why didn't you give her the 'special' kid? After all she already has three *normal* kids. Why does it have to be our kid?" he gritted his teeth in disgust.

"If you really exist, why would you let this happen to anyone?" he demanded. "Well, I'm not going to let this happen to us, I swear, I won't let *you* do this to us!" he said to himself while looking up into the abyss of low clouds hoping his ire reached all the way to God. "Smite me if you want to, I DON'T CARE!" he muttered but was shouting in his head.

He broke out into a trot which gave way to a full sprint which he didn't even realize until he'd reached the end of street. He stopped and stood there at the end of the street catching his breath contemplating where to go next when an odd thought came to him. He wasn't sure where he'd heard it. Most likely one of his real estate conventions but it struck him in one of those sudden revelation. *Whenever you're running toward one thing, you're running away from another but whether you run to achieve or from a fear of loss you can still reach your destiny.*

"Yeah, well my destiny is to have a normal son, not one with some chromosomal birth defect!" he said as if talking to someone though no one was there. He took a deep breath, turned and headed slowly back toward home.

CHAPTER EIGHT

Sinking

When Sara opened her eyes, they were dry and painful. No doubt bloodshot from the all of the crying she'd done the previous day and sporadically throughout the night. The skyline outside her window was dark. Hints of orange and red painted soft lines across the skyline as dawn approached. The faint glow of the street light highlighted some low clouds, the only contrast to the gloomy scene.

She sat up and reached into her nightstand drawer to retrieve some eye drops to soothe her burning eyes and clear her vision but it didn't seem to help much. A dull throb beat against her temple and the agony of the previous day had not eased. The muscles of her stomach ached; it felt like she'd been punched in the gut.

As she watched the night sky fade, the events at

the doctor's office seemed to be on a loop, forcing her to relive its pain again and again. Sara was being tormented by the onslaught of emotions. Why did she feel this way? She was quite familiar with the emotions but confused by the context. She had felt this way only once before. In the weeks that followed her mom's funeral.

How could she be grieving the death of someone who wasn't dead? She was perplexed by the experience. She knew her baby was still alive, growing in her womb. She had heard his heartbeat thumping away like a racehorse and she'd seen his smile. He was as real and alive as she was. The thought of it all brought on a fresh river of tears. *God, why? Why is this happening to my baby?* She looked up at the ceiling, silently begging for a response. "Why would you let this happen?" but there was no response, only silence.

Sara had grown up in a non-denominational church. They had always taught that God loved everyone and didn't cause sickness or disease, or in this case 'chromosomal birth defects'. The other prominent and repeated message was that Jesus could heal the sick even now, more than two-thousand years after his own death.

It always painted a hopeful picture for the hopeless but Sara wasn't usually hopeless. She considered herself a faithful believer in that message. But in that

room, in that moment, everything she'd ever believed
about God and Jesus, heaven and hell and the
certainty she'd had in all of it was, without warning,
pulled into a shadow of doubt bordering on disbelief.

She couldn't help her son and she knew it. That
helpless feeling drove the knife of despair deeper into
her heart which was now broken to the point of being
physically painful. She'd shut out the world and
wrapped herself in her grief and guilt. She was alone
and for now that's the way she wanted it. After all
what would she say to people? What could she say to
them so that they would understand what she was
going through?

Out of the blue, her phone rang out from her purse
which lay on the floor next to her nightstand,
startling her. She pulled her phone out and held it
up, squinting through her burning eyes to see who
was calling. It was her dad. Unsure of what she'd say
to him, slipped her finger over the 'decline' button
and lightly touched it. She waited for a few minutes,
soon her phone made a distinctive *ting* sound
indicating a message was left.

She wasn't sure she even wanted to listen to it but
her dad hadn't really gotten over her mom's passing
and she just needed to make sure he was okay. She
pressed the message button "Sara, it's dad. I was just
calling because, well, um… I just wanted to talk to
you honey. It's not urgent or anything but…

Anyway, I'll talk to you later. I love you." She hung
up the phone thinking *I'm sorry dad. I can't right now.*
You just wouldn't understand, I don't even understand. I
just... I just can't right now.

She stared at the walls trying to imagine the
conversation she might've had with her dad. *Hey dad,*
how are you? By the way, your grandson has Down
syndrome.

What? he would say *"Down syndrome? How'd that*
happen?

I don't know dad but it means he's... well he's not
going to be normal! she allowed herself the thought but
guilt instantly washed over her just for having it. She
bit her lower lip attempting to hold back the tears but
it was too late. She curled back into a fetal position
and wept. It wasn't long before she was asleep again,
exhausted from crying... and feeling.

Three hours had passed before she was awakened
by both the door bell and her phone ringing
simultaneously. She looked at her phone "Stacey...
no, no, no, no" she said as she peeked out the
window into the driveway. There sat Stacey's car.
No doubt she'd come to see if Sara was, "still alive
because I haven't heard from you for over a week" as
she would say.

Stacey was her best friend and confidante. It was
rare that they wouldn't talk or see each other every
couple of days or so. Especially after her mom died

Stacey had made sure that Sara was always taken care of and taking care of herself. Unlike many of her other friends, she stayed through some of the worst days while she'd tried to deal with her mom's passing. She was always trying to cheer her up, which most days was more annoying than anything else. Then one day Sara caught herself singing. The loss somehow seemed just a bit more bearable.

But Sara didn't want to be cheered up right now. She may have been trapped in her pain but for now it was familiar... almost comfortable. Plus she didn't want to go through the additional pain of having to explain her son's diagnosis or how she felt about it to anyone, not today, not even to her best friend. The truth was she was conflicted about how she felt and was struggling to make it all make sense. Sara silenced her phone and laid there for nearly half an hour enduring Stacey's persistent knocking and her phone lighting up from her constant calling. Suddenly it all stopped. Sara could hear the faint sound of a car door closing and Stacey driving slowly away. She felt relieved but slightly ashamed for ignoring Stacey. She knew she was just being a good friend.

As the time past her mind wandered. *Maybe the doctor was wrong...* she quickly dismissed the thought as not possible. The doctor explained that the amnio tests weren't right one hundred percent of the time but they were right often enough for the medical community to depend on them. Despite the advice of her dad always telling her to get a second opinion on the "heavy stuff", it wasn't something she even considered… at least not this time.

"If I wouldn't have wanted a baby so much and pushed Jacob to have one… maybe, just maybe this wouldn't be happening." She pondered the statement and heard Jacob's reaction even though he wasn't in the room "That's ridiculous! There was no way to know that!"

She was spiraling fast and she could feel it. *This is all Jacob's fault!* It was a fleeting thought she knew wasn't true. She loved Jacob more than anyone in the entire world but she was consumed by her own grief. She started to cry once more but she had spent all her tears; though her body continuing the gut wrenching motions of a now tearless weeping.

After contemplating every 'what if' situation she could conceive, she settled on one last thought: *God must be punishing me for something.* She looked up to heaven, "God, what did I do wrong?" she cried out. "What do you want from me?" she mumbled as she curled up once again allowing her loneliness and her mourning for her son to push her back into a silent trance. She lay there feeling more broken than she had ever felt before as she drifted back to sleep.

CHAPTER NINE

Searching

At the base of the stairs Jacob glanced back at the door and deliberated, considering whether or not returning to the bedroom again was a wise decision. It had been three days since they'd returned home with the devastating news and it was clear to him that Sara was hurting. *I hope she doesn't tailspin like she did after her mom,* he stopped himself from even thinking the rest of the thought. He knew that there was no witty charm he could offer that would be enough to help bounce her out of it, not this time.

Jacob needed a moment to clear his head before he let his frustration, which had quickly built up get the better of him. There had to be *something* that he could do. Somewhat flustered, he paced the floor until he noticed the bright red and white paper sticking out from under his wallet which he'd laid on top of his desk. Jacob pulled out the paper the doctor had given them and began skimming through it. In bright red letters the first words he read were *'variety of complications'* before reading the bold headings: **Heart Defects, Leukemia.** He looked up to consider the impact of those two words.

The words of the doctor rang loudly in his head *'There are no cures for chromosomal birth defects'*. It was like the clanging of a cymbal that grew louder and louder *no cure, no cure, no cure.* Was this some sort of cruel trick? Tears burned his eyes, though that was the last thing that he wanted to do.

His laptop lay open in front of him. An intense, almost demented curiosity seized him. He had to know what else could be potentially wrong with his son. Because he convinced himself 'that's the only way to prepare for what was coming, right?' He typed furiously: D*own syndrome heart defect statistics.* The top search result was from the National Down Syndrome Society and without opening the link he saw his answer in the summary. "Approximately half of all infants born with Down Syndrome have a heart defect." His mouth hung open in shock. "Half of them?" he said in disbelief, "Are you *kidding me?"*

Caught in a haze of questions he did another search for *Down Syndrome Leukemia statistics.* The results were less obvious but with a few clicks to different pages he landed on some official looking government website that said kids with Down Syndrome were ten to twenty times more likely to develop the disease than their normal counterparts. "This is insane..." He trailed off into a thought. *It's not just a simple chromosomal birth defect, it's almost guaranteed to be terminal.*

He started to backspace his search terms and stopped after he'd erased statistics and more bold words glared at him **Infectious Diseases, Dementia, Sleep Apnea.** A picture started to form in his mind, one of his son, him and Sara going through the agony of serious illnesses, developmental hurdles in a child who couldn't even understand what was happening to him. The thought of which overwhelmed Jacob. He tried desperately to swallow the huge lump in his throat. He quickly closed the computer screen to protect himself from the unbearable thoughts of his own son's suffering. He stood up and once again started to pace the floor.

He lifted the screen and moved the mouse over 'images' but hesitated. Do you really want to see this? No! he thought but his finger pressed down on the mouse. Hundreds of images populated the screen of children who looked sweet and innocent. He started to smile but caught himself, *don't you see what's wrong with them? It's obvious they're different than normal kids. What's wrong with you?* He quickly closed the web page hoping to quell his disturbing thoughts.

He picked up the brochure from the doctor again and skimmed through it until 'If you are pregnant you have options: Abortion, Adoption or Parenting'. He looked further down to the heading 'Abortion' and read on "24 weeks! That means if we want to end this thing we only have about six more weeks!"

Okay let's just think this through. You're a problem solver and this is a problem that just needs the right solution he thought. Jacob sat back down at his desk and pulled out a legal pad. He drew a line down the middle and on one side he wrote "pros" and the other "cons". It was a decision technique that had history all the way back to Ben Franklin and Jacob used it regularly to deal with difficult decisions.

He wrote 'keep the baby' across the middle of the page "Pros... we'd have a son. Um..." he sat tapping his pen on the paper trying to find another pro to write down. *Maybe I just need to get some of the cons out of my head* he thought. He wrote: Mentally slow, physically under developed, he'll look different, possibly heart problems, leukemia, seizures "That's just off the top of my head. I mean if I did more research I can't imagine what I could add to this list" he said.

He set the paper aside and pulled out another and repeated the process. At the top of the page he wrote 'end it and start over', then drew the line down the middle. Pros: No mental or physical delays, no one calling my son retarded, no death sentence, no cancer, no heart problems, no... he stopped writing. Cons: Getting Sara to agree, was all he wrote.

How the hell am I going to convince her to do that is just six weeks!?" it was more a statement than a question. "Really five weeks to convince her and one week to get it done. She won't even talk to me right now and if I can't talk to her how will I ever be able to convince her that this is best plan for *us*?"

He wracked his brain trying to see a clear path, some way to solve the problem. "If I could just find a way to talk to her I'll be able to make her see that she... no," he stopped himself to rephrase, "No... that *we* can't deal with all the complications of a baby with multiple medical problems. And that the doctor might be right, the best solution is to start over" he said it out loud to see if it sounded sensible because in his mind it made sense.

They had no other option. Surely this was more humane than allowing a baby that was predestined to live a life of illness to be born into the world. *We can't do it emotionally. We can't afford it financially. She'll see that the doctor is right. She has to. No one has to suffer here.* "Don't worry Sara, we can try again in a few months and have the baby you want... that we both want." Even as the words floated around in his head, he knew something wasn't right about them but they were all he could come up with in that moment.

Not wanting to upset Sara but wanting to try to draw her into having the unwanted conversation he knew he had to have a good reason to engage her. He recalled his mother talking to him recently that she'd started using homeopathic remedies. Was that was an option? Maybe they have something for her nausea or something.

He typed with purpose into the search engine again, this time writing *homeopathic remedies for nausea during pregnancy.* A list of products appeared at the top of the screen of pregnancy teas and ginger root. He read several of them and said "yes, a tea to settle the morning sickness... that could work. She'd have to sit up and talk to me. At least that way I could feel her out to see if she's receptive to the idea. Yeah, I'll do that."

He quickly pulled up their favorite vitamin store and found a tea that would suit his purpose. "I think this'll work." He popped out of his chair, grabbed his coat and headed for the door.

CHAPTER TEN
Signs

Jacob had just entered the freeway headed north toward town. It was clear right away that the late afternoon drive to the health food store, which usually took only fifteen minutes, would take much, much longer. "Oh, c'mon" he said frustrated as the traffic slowed just inching along only every few minutes. He looked to each lane to try to find a way out of his predicament but he was boxed in on all sides. "All I wanted to do is help my wife and you got to put up a literal road block! God, you're awesome!" he said speaking to Him sarcastically.

He clicked on the radio of the Lexus they had inherited from Sara's mom. It was one of the two gifts they'd received in the will. The other being her personal Bible complete with dog eared pages, passages highlighted in various colors, some

highlighted multiple times and the special penciled
notes in the margins. To Jacob, the car was the more
valuable of the two. When he looked up from finding
the volume button, he was just a few feet from the car
in front of him. His foot instinctively jumped to the
brakes to avoid the impending fender bender. The
last thing Jacob needed was to wreck this car. For
months after her passing, Sara wouldn't let anyone
drive the car, not even herself. She would only sit in
it because it made her feel closer to her mom. Images
of Sara's response to the news that he'd wrecked,
dinged or even scratched her mom's car made the
hair on the back of his neck stand straight up.

He took a deep breath and held the brake before
starting to flip through the stations looking for some
explanation for the sea of traffic he had been fighting
with. The DJ crackled through the fuzzy connection,
"And now: Traffic and weather from your favorite
radio station 97.5 THE JAM. It looks like
it's gonna be mostly cloudy skies with a high of forty-
two. It's gonna be a rough day for those traveling on
the East Loop, traffic is backed up all the way to
Memorial due to a major accident. Reports of a
fatality and a police investigation are underway, so if
you can avoid the area do yourself a favor and do so.
Otherwise, you'd better pack some patience on your
drive to wherever life is taking you."

"Great, exactly what I needed," he said to himself,

not noticing his insensitivity. Patience had never been one of Jacob's strong suits, especially when he was driving. He hated traffic. All he could think about was how to get out of this man made captivity. He looked right and left over his shoulder to gauge his chances of bullying his way through.

"Oh my God!" He growled through clenched teeth. He slammed back into his seat and forced the car into park, defeated for the moment.

In his final act of rebellion he rolled the volume dial on the radio until it would go no further. The band 311 Down was playing on the radio, sending the speakers into a fit of pounding that threatened to inflict early deafness upon him. Begrudgingly, he pulled back the volume to a level less painful to his own ears but made sure it was still loud enough to be considered obnoxious to other drivers.

The only decipherable words in the song were *down, down* which seemed to direct his thoughts right back to the doctor's office and his son's diagnosis. *Down syndrome... I wonder why they call it that? Is it because those kids look down? Nah, it couldn't be that. The guy who discovered it, his name was probably Down something or something Down.* He paused to ponder his own question then shook his head to rid his thoughts of the inquiry. *It doesn't matter anyway, we can't handle life with a handicapped kid, it's as simple as that.* His throat thickened again as the pressure of the untapped well of emotions threatened to surface. He swallowed hard, played with the knob on the radio to prevent himself from feeling any kind of personal connection to their baby.

How am I going to do this? He wondered, drumming his hands on the steering wheel. Physical manifestations of his stress beaded across his forehead in the form of sweat. "I don't want to raise a kid who's mentally *challenged*! I mean, I don't want our kid to grow up being called retarded or worse a retard." He corrected himself, in an attempt to convince himself that he'd successfully changed his demeaning language. He knew that he had to get this right, otherwise it had the potential to blow up in his face in a big way. *But I need to convince Sara this is the right thing for us. So, you've got to choose your words carefully* Jacob thought to himself as the words of the doctor reverberated across his consciousness: *life full of challenges* and *end the pregnancy*.

Finally the far right lane of the freeway started to move. He quickly pulled the shifter into drive and began to inch toward the next lane. He successfully detoured onto the exit lane of the freeway. It wasn't long before he was within eye shot of what caused the parking lot on the freeway. A large delivery truck had a car pinned under its bed and the cabin of the car was visibly crushed. A white sheet was draped over the obvious victim of the incident that was mentioned on the radio earlier.

Jacob noticed the truck displayed a logo *Family Planning Centers of America* and had a picture of a Hispanic woman smiling, her bright white teeth depicting her celebration and just below her happy face were the words *helping women choose their own path through women's health options.*

Jacob thought it was odd that he'd noticed the truck or its message. Those things usually escaped him completely even though they never did Sara. *If we were wandering a barren desert together she'd be the one to spot its only oasis,* he thought. The truck's message seemed to wash over him consoling him in some way as if to say, "You know the right answer but just in case I left you a message."

With that, he felt right. Like he'd received some mystical confirmation that his plans were the right ones. "It's the only solution," he mumbled. "But... Sara, she's not just going to accept this 'sign from the universe' as a good enough reason."

He started to rehearse in his mind all the plausible explanations that sounded like good enough reasons to follow the doctor's advice.

The risk for complications were high, he thought before saying, "I could show her all the articles I found. Who's not going to take the Mayo Clinic's word for it, right?" He asked himself and then affirmed his question by shaking his head.

"We don't want to watch the baby suffer through something like Leukemia or something worse and then just watch him die." He said and then recalibrated the statement to make it more palatable for Sara. *I'll just ask her: could you handle it if the baby developed Leukemia or worse?* Make sure you pause before you say "or worse" he thought as if he were developing a sales presentation. And he knew that she would take his question the rest of the way; her picturing herself at the funeral, sobbing uncontrollably. "That's what I'll tell her" he said. *I hope its enough* he thought.

He made it to the health food store and bought two boxes of the herbal tea before heading home taking an alternative route to avoid any further delays from the accident. By the time he pulled back into their driveway it was ominously dark out. He sat in the car for several minutes as he went over the conversation, playing both roles in his head multiple times. Now that he was home, he was beginning to feel the weight of his plan bearing down on him.

CHAPTER ELEVEN

Nausea Tea

The diagnosis meant many things to Jacob. At best the baby would be born with mental challenges and at worst, life or the universe or God would sentence him to death by leukemia or heart defect or whatever other catastrophic diagnoses were attached to Down syndrome. Jacob prepared the anti-nausea tea for Sara as he had been doing everyday for two weeks. He knew they were running out of time if they were to act on ending the pregnancy and starting over. And he had even less time to convince her to consider, then follow through on the plan. He had contemplated the options in front of him and it didn't matter which way the cards were dealt, the thought of any of them was unbearable to consider, even for him.

His research on Down syndrome had only made

the hope of his son having a remotely decent life fade away. The images of babies on ventilators and bald heads or undergoing complex heart surgeries had etched themselves into his consciousness and only solidified his decision. *This is our only real option* he thought "I just want to spare all of us, even this poor helpless baby, from a life filled with doctors, hospitals or worse. It's is the right thing for us to do!" He said to himself bitterly, torn by his own sea of emotions. He wasn't sure who he was trying to convince anymore - Sara or himself.

He carried the tea upstairs and cautiously tapped on the bedroom door before inching it open "Are you awake?" he spoke into the darkened room. The curtains were closed so that the only thing he could see was her silhouette, dark and undefined.

"Yeah, I'm awake." She hadn't been out of the bed much since they got home from the doctor's office. She'd hadn't eaten much either but when she eventually did she'd have to force herself to and she did it only for the baby's benefit.

"I was just checking on you..." He said gently brushing his free hand against her cheek. The pain she was going through was evident. Her anguish was written into every worried crease on her forehead. "I brought you some of your pregnancy tea." He held up the mug with the warm tea. "This will make you feel better, babe, I promise," he said as cheerfully as he could manage. An authentic sense of husbandly duty to help and protect her drove him. To him, he was doing the right thing.

"I really don't want to drink that, it tastes funny" she said looking up from underneath their plush covers. Her dark brown hair fell in untidy waves over her eyes which did everything but conceal the confused pain in them.

"I know honey but the people at the vitamin store said it'll help you with the morning sickness. Plus they said it'll help keep your strength up and help you feel better" he insisted, rubbing circles on her back.

"Fine" she reluctantly agreed pushing herself into a sitting position. It took her a moment, pressing her hand to her temple, obviously pushing away an ache of some kind. Jacob couldn't decide whether it was emotional or physical so he remained expressionless.

"So, how are you feeling?" he probed again handing her the cup.

"I guess I feel okay..." She attempted a grin for his benefit. She lifted the warm cup to her lips, wrinkling her nose in distaste. "This smells awful too" she complained.

"It can't be that bad," Jacob laughed nervously, knowing that he was walking into the lion's den of subject matter. There was a brief pause before he continued. "That's good because there's something I was hoping to talk to you about but only if you're up to it..."

The way he let the sentence trail off made Sara noticeably tense. She shifted her weight slightly and waited patiently for him to continue. Jacob's plan was to test the water to see if she would be even remotely receptive to what he was saying. This required him to tread lightly because he knew how tightly Sara held to her religious beliefs.

Although they attended church, they weren't active members. They casually attended when the holidays called for it or when Sara was feeling particularly guilty for having been absent for a long time. But that was because of Jacob. Sara had grown up going to church and her faith was ingrained into her DNA as much as stubbornness was ingrained into his. Jacob's upbringing was such a contrast to hers. His dad's religion was his work and his mom preferred cleaning the house on Sundays. Jacob had a little of both his parents in him, so Sara graciously accommodated him by watching their local church services online most Sundays.

It wasn't often that their personalities clashed so much that it led to a heated fight but when they did they made sure to include saying all the hurtful things they would later regret. Jacob had a surging uneasiness in his stomach that indicated to him that this conversation had the potential of becoming just that an explosive fight.

She was raised in a modest, conservative home where abortions were in no uncertain terms an act of murder. Jacob remembered this in painful detail, recalling one of their first Thanksgivings as a married couple. The television had flashed briefly to a local news story about a couple who'd had multiple abortions but refused to use birth control. The story had sparked major controversy amongst pro-life and religious groups on one side and pro-abortion and women's choice groups on the other. Brashly, Jacob had piped up, "Who cares?" Sara's eyes had turned to saucers, and her father's face reddened as he passionately delivered an hour long lecture about why he should care and how wrong abortion was. Too which Jacob concluded that he was likely a religiously eccentric or maybe a little crazy.

That was why Jacob had to walk on eggshells around this subject. Sara was a lot like her father in the sense that you couldn't convince her something was right if she believed it to be wrong. He wasn't sure how she'd react to it because he had vowed never to bring up the subject again after that awkward Thanksgiving dinner but he was betting that she held very similar views to her family and was possibly as passionate about it as her dad.

Generally he didn't agree with abortion but had

never really given it that much thought. He certainly didn't go out of his way to discuss the subject, except when he was pressed. He'd always allowed for a few exceptions for rape, incest and of course the mother's health. But now, it had become a real issue to him that under these circumstances was instantly filled with gray areas.

To him, this was an act of mercy, not an exception to some hard and fast rule. He was bracing himself for her reaction, already responding in his mind with statements like, "It's nearly the same as helping someone end it when they're suffering and dying of cancer." He took a step towards the foot of the bed, turning away from her momentarily.

"What is it?" Sara asked after too much time had passed. The room had gotten thick with anticipation, it loomed over them like the dark clouds of an impending thunderstorm. He knew that this was the calm and once the words escaped his lips, there would be no turning back. It would be straight into the storm from there.

"Did you finish your tea?" he asked to buy enough time to gather his thoughts before he spoke.

She gulped it down and then showed him the empty cup.

Jacob felt the moisture in his mouth disappear, leaving his lips dry, "Well, uh-um" he cleared his throat, "After you left the doctor's office when we got

the news about the baby he said
something... something I think we should talk
about."

"What? What did he say?" she demanded hoping
for a glimmer of good news.

"Just take a deep breath, okay" he said as calmly as
he could, "It's just that--"

"Just what?" she said, clearly distressed and
running out of patience with him for beating around
the bush.

"Okay, I don't know how to say this any other way
so... I'll just tell you exactly what he said." He paused
one last time "The doctor explained to me that the
Down syndrome most likely won't be the only
problem we might have to deal with."

"What does that mean?" She responded
defensively. Alarms were going off in Jacob's head,
he was too focused to realize he should've stop
talking.

"The doctor mentioned it and then I did some
research on it, too. They call it a chromosomal birth
defect and kids with it have other more serious
issues. For example, I read how half of them also
have heart defects, others have seizures. And that
these kids are 20 times more likely to get
Leukemia." His voice sounded automated, like a kid
in middle school who was spouting facts he'd just
memorized.

"Leukemia?" She repeated blankly.

He allowed the words to settle into her imagination and he knew it wouldn't be long before she began imagining the possibilities. Something restless stirred inside of him, guilt he banished to the back of his mind. It was too late to go back and he was committed to his plan, *This is for your own good* he thought as he waited to continue.

Her brown eyes welled with tears again, as she had barely recovered from the week of roller coaster emotions and sobbing sessions. He knew he had accomplished what he had set out to do.

Feeling confident she was in the state of mind he'd expected her to be in he continued, "The doctor told me that if we weren't prepared for a lifetime of challenges, not just for *us* but for this *baby*" he paused to give the appropriate emphasis, "then we should consider ending this pregnancy and trying again in a few months." There. It was out there.

The already tense atmosphere intensified. The only sound he could hear was his heartbeat pounding in his ears, as he awaited her response. It was some time before she reacted. Her demeanor had dramatically changed and her words snapped out of her like a whip cutting the air "Oh really? And what do *you* think?"

"Hold on now, we're just talking this out." He held his hands up defensively, feeling the full force of her words.

She just stared hard into her hands which lay in her lap and waited. "I think," again he hesitated. He knew it was too late, he had to press his case now so he exhaled heavily and said, "I think we should seriously consider what the doctor said and make a responsible decision." There he'd said it and for a moment he felt somewhat relieved.

"Make a responsible decision?" Sara couldn't hide the sound of betrayal in her voice. She had never been good at concealing her feelings. She looked up from her hands and back at Jacob looking for understanding, eyebrows furrowed in a mixture of pain, confusion and anger. "Didn't you hear our baby's heartbeat?" she asked with her hand atop of her belly "How can we even consider…" she paused searching for the right word "… *that.*" She couldn't bring herself to say it out loud.

"I know that we heard the heartbeat but honey… the doctor told me that baby can't feel anything yet and if we're going to do something we should do it soon. I know this isn't a conversation you want to have right now but I think we need to have it and honestly I think…" He sounded as desperate as he felt. Getting Sara to see reason had always been his greatest challenge that often led to conflicts with her. All he wanted to do was make the right decision for them, for their family.

"Is that what *YOU* want to do?" she challenged, her arms crossed over her chest.

"I think it's the right thing to do, yes. It's like helping a person with cancer..." he started into his prepared explanation.

Her face turned flush and then fiery, her mind was visibly looking for words. She screamed out interrupting him, "You want me to kill my baby!"

"Why do you always take things to the extreme?" he asked but it was more a statement to reflect his dissipating patience. "I'm trying to prevent this kid from having to live a life of misery and possibly a horrific death! I call that mercy not murder!" Now, angry he said, "What about you, do you honestly think you could watch your own baby die a slow, painful death and not go nuts? Right now that baby only has Down syndrome and that alone is sending you over the edge."

Sara launched into full wailing before he realized the impact of his words. He took several deep breaths before trying to pull back, "I didn't mean that. I'm just saying that I think it'll be hard... maybe too hard, to raise a kid who has mental deficiencies" he said pointedly.

"Are you calling our son retarded? How could you call our baby retarded?" she growled through gritted teeth, indignant.

"I didn't say retarded, I said mental deficiencies

and it's the truth... he'll be mentally challenged" and I don't want a son like that!" he blurted out instantly regretting his words.

CHAPTER TWELVE

Backfire

"How could you even think that?" Now she was properly offended. It felt a little like a self-fulfilling prophecy. He was drowning in his own sea of unmanaged emotions: regret, frustration, anger - at God, himself, at his unborn, imperfect son. Even at Sara.

"I was thinking the same thing about you!" he said obnoxiously. So *much for graciously bowing out*, he thought.

Tears flowed freely as she mumbled to herself, flabbergasted by his response, "But he's our baby."

"What! What'd you say?" he said angrily.

The effect of his words were immediate. She glared at him, "I said *'he's our baby!'*"

In all his years of real estate sales training he'd

84

learned about emotional attachment. And he knew that by her statement, she'd already built an emotional connection with the baby too strong for him to unravel. And she'd made the connection in spite of the pain she was experiencing because of his diagnosis.

That connection threatened the plan that Jacob had so carefully laid out in his mind. As he watched it fall apart in front of him, all he could think was *She's being too emotional to see the truth.*

She was shutting down and he knew if he wanted to redeem any part of this conversation he had to think fast. He took a deep breath waited a few moments and said very calmly. "You heard what the doctor said. The baby is most likely going to have serious challenges. Do you want it to have to go through life like that?"

"It! So, our baby is just an 'it' to you?" She spat so fiercely that a vein was protruding from her temple.

He wiped his face with the sleeve of his shirt. "That's not what I meant, honey," he murmured trying to calm the now explosive situation. "I just meant that I don't want 'our baby' to suffer. And what if the doctors are right and he has other problems, too. I just think we should consider all our options."

"Yeah, what you and that doctor want to do is to kill my baby! You can just forget it. Just LEAVE ME

ALONE!" she shouted as loud as she could before covering her face with her hands.

Jacob walked around the bed and tried to gently pull her hands away so he could see her face. She jerked away from him and in defiance buried her head onto her pillow.

He took another drawn out breath and said calmly "You know I love you, at least you should after the last seven years and I know that we waited to have kids but we can have another..."

"Get out!!" she said sternly as she got up from the bed, intently walked past him as if she was going to leave the room.

He followed her into the hallway "Sara just calm down baby, calm down! I don't want to leave you like this. It's okay, we don't have to talk about this right now!" he bargained as she stopped a foot or so out the door. Once he was where she wanted him, she turned and walked back to their doorway and stood there. "C'mon, baby just calm down!"

"LEAVE ME THE HELL ALONE! I'M NOT GOING TO KILL MY BABY, JACOB!" I mean it... just go! she yelled, taking one step backwards, she grabbed the door and slammed it in his face. Then she turned and leaned her back against the door and slid down to the floor all in one fluid motion. When she was sitting on the floor she looked up. A framed scroll with the words "*For I know the plans I have for you says the Lord, they are plans for good and not evil to give you a future and a hope"* Jeremiah 29:11 hung on the wall. She rebelliously thought, God, *what a load of crap, how is this a plan for my good!?*

Jacob tapped on the door. "Honey, please open the door and let's talk about this, okay?"

She reached up to the door knob, locked the door and said to him firmly: "Jacob, I'm done. I don't want to talk to you now. I don't want to talk to you about this ever again! You don't want our baby: that's all I needed to know. Go away."

"Sara, don't do this!" he said through the small crack in the door. But Sara didn't respond, "Sara…. Sara, you have to talk to me!" he tried again. He could feel his face start to burn. *How dare she treat me like this when all I'm trying to do is protect her?* "Sara, DAMN IT! Stop being so dramatic and open the door!" he shouted.

A single piece of paper suddenly came from under the door and lay at his feet. It read: *I can't look at you right now and I can't stand the sound of your voice. Leave now.*

His anger had boiled over, he clenched the paper in his fist and hit the door shouting through it, "Fine, that kid is going to be defective… and… and you can have it all to yourself!" he instantly felt remorse for his choice of words as they echoed back at him from against the door "I'm sorry, I didn't mean that. Sara, did you hear me? I didn't mean that. Please don't do this!" he said. Deep down he knew it was too late, the imprisoned words had escaped his thoughts and wreaked their havoc.

Why can't she see I'm trying to help her? he thought stubbornly as he walked down the stairs. He stopped midway down the stairs, taking a step back up wondering "What am I gonna do now?" He thought about going back and kicking the door down but the image of paramedics, hospitals and him in handcuffs being hauled away to jail prevented him from pursuing his impulse.

Sara listened carefully as the garage door opened and the tires squealed against the street as Jacob quickly sped away. She didn't care this time. "My baby is all that matters now," she said brushing her fingers against her stomach. Not even all the powers of hell would prevent her from protecting this baby.

Confident that Jacob was gone and wouldn't come back she climbed into the bed still wearing the same clothes she wore to the doctor's office. She pulled the covers up over her head and closed her eyes willfully trying to escape her own thoughts.

CHAPTER THIRTEEN

Checking In

The morning light was beginning its daily conquest over the bluish black sky as Jacob pulled into the parking lot of the hotel. He parked as close to the entrance as he could, the night sky lit only by the golden glow of the parking lights. The biting air of north winds swirled around Jacob as he opened the car door. Hurried by the chill of the wind he slammed the car door shut, pushed the alarm button on his key-chain and headed for the front entrance.

He'd been driving around all night with no particular destination. The silence of the car, the hum of the tires gripping the road and flashing of the white stripes as he pressed on the accelerator created the perfect setting in which to lose himself. His fury had given way to the silent struggle of his feelings but the long night of endless soul searching had resulted in nothing but utter exhaustion.

Jacob pulled his overcoat closed in a vain attempt to counter the chill that was creeping down his spine. He walked with purpose up the shallow wheelchair ramp to the door that held the salvation of central heating. Reaching for the door he paused to see a young boy inside slowly walking toward him. There was something odd about him that captivated Jacob - maybe it was the curious slant in his eyes or the unreadable expression on his face. Jacob shook himself from his thoughts and yanked the first door. Nothing happened. It was locked.

The boy, who appeared to be a teen, maybe even a little younger was headed to the other door. Jacob did a slight side step, grabbing the handle of the door to allow the boy to exit. It freed up the doorway for him to enter and for Jacob to get a better look at him.

"Thank you sir!" the boy said happily.

Jacob was too taken aback to reply. He tried to speak but words failed him. It was the way the boy spoke that surprised him. It seemed different, almost out of place. It wasn't the words themselves, which on the surface seemed a perfectly natural response but the over the top enthusiasm in his voice that contradicted the strange, almost sad look on his face.

"Thank you sir!" the boy repeated, breaking Jacob from his trance long enough for him to reply.

"No problem," Jacob said as the boy walked past. He entered the building feeling a weird sense of familiarity. *That was strange... I must be tired,* Jacob concluded. He looked back at the door almost wishing to catch another glimpse at the boy when his attention was redirected.

"Good morning, can I help you sir?" an elderly man appeared in front of him from behind the counter, wearing a red and black flannel shirt which he had buttoned all the way up until it disappeared under his long white beard.

"Oh, um… yes, I uh… I need a room please." He replied.

"For how long?"

"Um, well that's a good question." He said as the heaviness of the question sank in. After a momentary pause to contemplate the question he said to the clerk, "I guess we'll take it one day at a time for now."

"Lady troubles?" the clerk asked.

"No, um… Oh forget it! Is it really that obvious?" Jacob laughed nervously, running a hand through his hair.

"I've been around a while. Was a bartender before this, so you aren't the first troubled face I've come across." The clerk explained. "I'll tell you what I'll do. You can pay day to day and if you're here for the week, I'll give you the discounted rate. How's that sound?"

"I really appreciate that Mister." He said gratefully.

"Whatever I can do to help is what I always say. I just need to see your driver's license and a major credit card to get you set up."

Jacob retrieved the requested items and tossed them onto the counter. As he waited for the clerk to enter his information into the computer, his thoughts began to race. He replayed the events of the last twenty-four hours again and again in his mind, like a movie clip on repeat. Every scene carrying its own weight. It distracted him making him mumble his responses.

"Uh-umm" the clerk said looking at him curiously.

Realizing how crazy he must have looked he said, "It's been a rough night and I need some sleep."

"Well, your room is ready." He replied. "I put you up on the 3rd floor in room 21. You can take the guest elevators around the corner or the stairs at the end of the hallway."

Normally, Jacob would have taken the stairs (if for no other reason than to claim that he did, in fact, exercise). As exhausted as he was, climbing the stairs seemed too great a task, so he opted to take the easy way out. He let out a long, ragged breath as he stepped into the empty compartment. The underpowered elevator inched higher making the ride feel much longer than it was. He fought desperately to keep his eyes open as the elevator finally came to a stop and the doors squeaked open. Stepping off he stood in front of the sign with convenient arrows pointing the way which read: *Rooms 1 to 11* and an arrow pointing down the hall to his left and then *Rooms 12 to 21* with an arrow pointing to the right.

He started down the hallway but to his pleasant surprise room 21 was the first door on the right. "Thank you mister clerk man," he said as he slid his key in and pushed the door open.

The curtains were open to expose and the eastern skyline, glowing with the cities lights reflected off the low cloud cover. He went straight for the bed dropping his trench coat on the floor. Without noticing a single detail of the room he collapsed face first onto the queen sized bed. His eyes shuttered for a moment with images of Sara looking back accusingly at him before giving into his exhaustion.

CHAPTER FOURTEEN

Finding Sara

Jacob's eyes popped open and all he could see in the darkness, was the amber glow of the clock on the nightstand. "Sara" he said before realizing he was in the hotel room. "Damn, why couldn't this all have been just a bad dream?"

He pushed himself up to sit and stared out at the city lights "What am I doing? I can't just walk away from the last seven years. No way, I need to talk to Sara," he said. He picked up the phone and started to pull up her number. Reprimanding himself, "wait, wait, what are you thinking? You can't talk to her on the phone about this. This is a conversation that requires a face-to-face."

He jumped up and headed out the door to the elevators and pushed the button to go down. His impatience got the better of him so he turned and

headed down the hallway, down the stairs and out
the side door. He quickly jumped in his car and sped
out of the parking lot.

He got lost in the scenery of the drive and his
thoughts flitted between Sara, the baby and how he'd
ended up on a winding road in the mountains. The
drive should've taken hours but seemed to only take
only several minutes. *Man, how in the world did I get
here so quickly?* he thought before quickly dismissing
it as him being inattentive.

Within minutes he was pulling into the garage at
home. As he entered the house the air seemed grave
and the shadows menacing. He walked slowly to the
stairs using all of his senses to tune into his
surroundings. *Something's wrong,* he thought. He
hurried up the stairs careful not to make any noise.

He carefully opened the door to their bedroom
expecting to find Sara lying in bed but the scene
frightened him. The lamp on her nightstand had
been pushed onto the floor and the lampshade lay
crumpled on the floor next to it. He hurried to the
bed where the covers had been pulled back "Oh
no… no Sara!" he cried out. "Sara, honey where are
you?" he shouted again and again. He ran down the
hall way shattering the silence. "Sara, where are
you?"

He darted to the nursery and threw the door open,
inspected the room but nothing was out of order. He

repeated his furious search through each room of the
house before returning to the bedroom and the bed.
His world turned black and white except for a pool
of red that consumed a large portion of the mattress.
"What have I done?" he cried out.

Suddenly the colors of the room returned to him
and he refocused on finding Sara. He pulled out his
phone and called the hospital. "Yes, I'm trying to
find out if my wife was admitted. She pregnant and I
think something's wrong, there's blood here. It's
everywhere and I can't find her..." he spoke
frantically.

"No sir, we haven't had any emergencies like that
but what's your wife's name?"

"Sara Michaels."

The phone went silent for a moment "I'm sorry,
sir, no one by that name came in. If there's an
emergency you should call 911." Multiple pulses of
light cut through the darkness followed a few
seconds later by the reverberated sound of thunder.

Jacob quickly hung up the phone and dialed 911.
Putting the phone up to his ear he waited for it to
connect but nothing happened. He pulled the phone
away and examined it and immediately identified the
problem.

No signal. "Are you kidding me!" he demanded
"What the hell is going on here?" He hung up and
dialed again. He tried moving around but nothing

changed. "Oh my God!" he exclaimed before rushing back to the garage, getting in his car and speeding away searching for a signal.

"Aw forget it!" he shouted as he slammed the phone into the passenger's seat. *Where would she go?* He wondered. "Stacey's" he announced. "Now how do I get to her house without my phone?" He had no choice but to drive to Stacey's house by memory. He had to find out if Sara was there.

It wasn't long before Jacob reached the freeway entrance and quickly exited onto its open road. Smashing down the accelerator as he reached the main lanes, he didn't even notice as the needle pushed past 60, then 70 and then 80 and he didn't care as the white stripes of the road soon blurred into a single line. All he could think about was finding Sara and his mind was had already taken him to every dark place the fear of the unknown could conjure up.

When he'd reached the other side of town on the loop, he found the exit he was looking for "222 bypass that's the one" he said as he slowed and made the exit. He exited at more than a speed that Sara would've found acceptable. He barreled down the road anxiously trying to reach his destination.

Because of his speed a relatively minor curve in the road caught him by surprise. He pushed down hard on the brakes and turned his wheel sharply to the right narrowly missing a ditch two feet deep on the other side of the street. He breathed a sigh of relief as he looked up from the ditch and down the road.

Lights.

Brighter and brighter they pursued him until they swallowed him. He cried out "Saraaaa!"

Jacob shot straight up in a panic, beads of sweat had begun to pool on his forehead and run down his face. The surroundings weren't immediately familiar to him but it wasn't long before he oriented himself, realizing where he was "My God it was just a dream!?" It was a question as much as a statement. He took a deep breath "It was just a dream" he said now both confused and relieved. He took a minute to survey his surroundings.

It was still dark outside the only light in the room was the soft red glow of the clock on the nightstand. The time read 1:23. "Too late to call her now," he said thinking of Sara. He picked up his phone pushed a button and brought it to life. He pulled up her number and stared at her picture. It was a picture he'd taken of her on their last vacation to Belize. Her eyes were slightly squinted and she was smiling, her head tilted back. It was one of his favorite pictures of her. He wondered what she was doing right then as he was thinking about her. Was she thinking about him or still wrestling with her pain? "I'll bet she's a mess, that's almost guaranteed" he said. *Maybe she's sleeping* and in that case he wouldn't want to wake her.

"Why hasn't she called me? Doesn't she care where I am?" he said as the offense of her rejection that drove him to the hotel in the first place was reignited. He loved her deeply and wanted to take care of her but her rejection was his kryptonite. "Whatever!" he said crossly. He turned the phone off and tossed it onto the nightstand. Laid his head back and stared at the ceiling.

An intense weariness overtook him. He tried to get up but he didn't seem to have the strength. His vision tunneled and the glow of the clock vanished. Everything, even his thoughts disappeared into the abyss of exhaustion.

CHAPTER FIFTEEN

Hunger Strikes

The bed was cold and empty. She ached for the warmth of Jacob's body snuggled against hers. Her tears had long since been spent the night before. Sara lay in her bed motionless, the weight of her shambled marriage and the prospect of a future raising her baby alone seemed too much to contend with. Every thought she entertained only deepened her sadness.

She tried to imagine her life without her son, the one she'd have if she did what Jacob and the doctor suggested and ended her pregnancy for the prospects of a better baby someday. "It's what he wants," she whispered. An image of an aborted fetus she'd seen once while passing an anti-abortion protest assaulted her mind before she tossed her head side to side shaking away the pictures and the pain that came with them. "I can't... I just can't, don't you understand?" She said talking to a conjured up image she created of Jacob.

He was gone and it bothered her that she didn't know where he was. She still loved him deeply. "I guess my love isn't enough for him to want our baby," she said while recounting their fight. Suddenly, she felt her stomach turn sour. She hung her head over the bed pulling the waste basket close to her face. She heaved but nothing happened. She wasn't surprised because her diet of late had consisted of nibbles of this and that with nothing substantial. When she ate anything, she did it out of obligation but not hunger.

She felt immersed in heartache and sorrow. She was wounded by his absence and it was only becoming more painful the longer she was isolated. She longed for Jacob and the security in his embrace. She imagined herself wrapped firmly in his iron grip, the hum of his voice ringing in her ears as she nestled further into his chest. It seemed an inviting cure for the pain but she knew that wasn't possible. She'd exhausted her remaining energy making him leave and for now she didn't have the reserves to push back against his unrelenting pressure again. She feared that in her desperation for comfort, her resolve would crumble and she would agree to his wishes against her own.

She reached into her nightstand to get a tissue but

something else caught her attention. It was the 4D picture from the sonogram they'd gotten from the doctor at their ultrasound appointment. She pulled it out slowly.

Enchanted by the images, she just took it all in. Thoughts of what their baby would look like lifted her spirits ever so slightly. She pictured her baby with different facial features and the color of his hair. In that moment of maternal bliss it occurred to her that she couldn't recall what a baby with Down syndrome really looked like. She knew they had some physical differences. She tried to form the picture of her son in her mind with the added features of a person with Down syndrome but she'd only seen people who had it in passing. *I guess it's not something you really go out of your way to understand... unless you're dealing with it yourself, like I am now* she thought.

Glancing back down at the sonogram picture she noticed an arrow pointing at a specific spot. She focused on the word typed across the bottom 'BOY'. "It's a boy! Our baby boy!" a smile cracked the gloom that had occupied her face as she instantly recalled the moment. For just a moment her sadness melted away and was replaced with the joyous memories of her and Jacob finding out they were having a baby boy.

"Jacob, it's a--" she started to call out but the echo

of her voice promptly subdued her elation. Her eyes burned at the fresh wound that her circumstances had become.

As she put all of her attention back on the sonogram and those three letters, she smiled. She couldn't believe she'd forgotten the arrow, it'd been such a big deal when they found out they were having a boy. Unexpectedly, she realized she was hungry. It was as if her little boy was crying out to her from her womb "I'm hungry, Mommy."

She took a deep breath to muster her strength before she stood and walked to the door and headed downstairs. As she entered the kitchen her eyes were immediately drawn to the wooden bowl on the prep island in the center of the room. Bananas, blackened by oxidation didn't dissuade her. She hurried to them, laid the sonogram photo down, picked up the bunch, peeled one and devoured it in just three bites.

She felt a rush of energy flood her body. She walked a few more steps to the stainless steel refrigerator in the corner of the kitchen. A magnet clung on the door but it held nothing. She retrieved the sonogram from the island and placed it on the refrigerator door, positioning it as if it were a Picasso painting before she secured it in place with the magnet. She stood back looking, satisfied with her placement she opened the door and pulled out anything and everything that looked remotely appetizing and feasted on it. She demolished some left over Mahi Mahi without reheating it. She tore into a cucumber, and a couple bites of Greek yogurt before she ended her binge with pickles and an ice cream sandwich savoring each and every bite.

Exhausted by her attack on the fridge, she sat on one of the breakfast bar stools facing the living room losing herself in thought. After some time she laid her head down on the bar. And with her stomach full, her eyes felt just as heavy. "Was that good?" she said talking to her son. He fluttered in her belly making her smile.

CHAPTER SIXTEEN

A Boy Named Alex

Dawn's light penetrated the room, its intensity mounting a full assault on Jacob, piercing his eyelids and interrupting his sleep. His eyes fluttered open trying to adjust to the brightness that now surrounded him. He turned over on his side, flipping the pillow under his head over his face, hoping to revisit his dreams. He squeezed his eyes shut trying to recall the picture of him and Sara.

Sleep had invited him back in time to the club where he and Sara had met. It was a happier time, when his biggest concern was whether or not they had enough time to squeeze in one more dance. Her face was so bright, so vibrant with joy. There was nothing in that moment but the two of them. All the pain that now gripped them didn't exist. It didn't even occur to him that in reality he hated to dance and only really did it to make Sara happy, which back then was easy to do. Now he'd gladly trade a million dances in the most uncomfortable shoes in the world if all of this would just go away.

Morning had won the battle over his dreams. He wasn't sure how long it had been but he felt groggy and unstable. He sat up and rubbed his eyes, stretching until he could feel the tension in his muscles release their hold. It wasn't long before his mind betrayed him completely with a full onset of memories of Sara sharp words. So sharp that they cut all the way to his heart.

He sat on the edge of the bed staring at the wall, the sunlight still making him squint. "What have I done? Sara... I really made a mess of things this time." he said regretfully.

He reminded himself: *You know you can't raise that kid. He's going to have problems, lots of them... he's not normal.* He felt guilty for feeling the way he did but he knew he was right. "I can't, I just can't!" he said putting his head in his hands. "How can I be the dad of a kid that's not normal? There's just no way I'd be a good enough dad to handle that many problems."

A light tapping at the door interrupted him from his internal dialogue. He tried to ignore the interruption but the tapping persisted.

Tap, tap, tap. Followed by a few seconds of silence and then tap, tap, tap.

Jacob called out, "Not now, I'm not dressed" he lied thinking it was the maid service but the tapping continued.

Jacob was now visibly frustrated and stomped toward the door, flinging it open. "Hey!" he began to say but the hallway in front of his door was empty. He stepped out, keeping one foot propped against the door and looked toward the elevators but there was no one there.

"I'm very sorry, Mister," a voice quietly said from the hallway directly behind him, startling him. His foot bracing the door slipped and was pinched between the door and its frame. He winced in pain pushing the door off with his hand.

He turned toward the voice and a boy stood several feet away smiling. It wasn't just a typical smile it was like the boy's whole face was lit up in a smile. His tongue protruded slightly past his teeth and his nose flush against his face. His eyes shaped like little almonds beamed with the excitement. "Today is March twenty-first and I wanted to offer you today's paper." The boy said with a lisp or so Jacob presumed but after more careful examination decided it was more like an accent.

Jacob peered at him quizzically but didn't reply. "It's free today." The boy added.

Jacob rebounded from gawking and finally replied "Sure, I'll take one." He held out his hand and retrieved the neatly folded paper.

Regretting scaring the boy Jacob asked "What's your name kid?"

"Alex" he replied.

"Well, thank you for the paper Alex" raising the paper and saluting him with it.

"You're welcome Mister, see you tomorrow!" Alex said as he started back down the hallway, his slightly opened backpack hauling the load of newspapers he was delivering for the day.

"In that case, call me Jacob!" He cupped his hand around his mouth in an attempt to direct his voice toward Alex.

Alex was nearly to the end of the hall and he replied "Okay, d…" but his voice trailed off.

"What was that?" Jacob shouted back.

Alex turned, smiled brightly and waved with one hand, like a hiker trying to be spotted in the wilderness. Then he simply turned and disappeared at the end of the hall.

Jacob peered curiously down the hallway hoping Alex would reappear but the hallway remained deserted. Jacob slipped back into his room. The glare of the sun now dimmed leaving the soft yellow glow of morning in its place. When he laid the paper on the table that was situated in the corner of the room, the headline caught his attention:

Boy With Down Syndrome Stuns World With

Beethoven-esque Symphony

He read on:

Andrew Bernstein, music director of the Mountain Fork Symphony, wowed the audience when he played a new symphonic piece that has been described as "Beethoven-esque". He stunned his audience when he introduced the composer who wrote the piece, a 13 year old boy with Down syndrome. Bernstein was quoted as saying "I know that this may seem an impossible task for such a boy who the world says is limited by his challenges. I suppose there were those who said the same about the deaf Ludwig Van Beethoven before he composed his 9th symphony. This boy is proving to the world that having a disability doesn't make one disabled but rather uniquely positions him to fulfill his God given destiny!"

Jacob looked at the picture that accompanied the article which showed a boy wearing a baseball cap. "It can't be." He said intensifying his focus on the boy. "It looks just like…." He turned and looked at the door and then looked back at the paper. "Why does this kid look familiar?" he searched his thoughts trying to remember "I'm sure I've met him somewhere but where?" he said unable to answer the question.

He read the entire article hoping to find out who the boy was, to confirm if his suspicions were true.

But the article said only that the boy's identity was being withheld for his protection. Puzzled, Jacob leaned back in the chair and his mind drifted "Is that even possible?" he wondered aloud.

His thoughts refocused on Sara. He noticed his cell phone on the table "I don't remember putting that there. But who knows? I could hardly think straight when I got here." He picked it up and pulled up Sara's cell number before he paused. *What would I even say to her?* he thought. From the depths of his mind a voice screamed in his head, *she doesn't want to talk to you! I'll bet she doesn't even answer your call, she hates you right now so why waste your time?* He pushed the button to dial the number.

Ring... ring... ring... click "You've reached Sara, I'm not able" Jacob hung up the phone.

"It only rang three times, she must've declined the call" he put the phone down, the gravity of how badly he had hurt her started sinking in. He had always prided himself on being a gifted communicator. He had piles upon piles of sales awards that proved it but *you can't even talk to your wife? Man, you must be the worst husband in the world.* The sadness he felt was quickly replaced with anger. Not at Sara but himself. And *this is the price for hurting her.*

What made Jacob such a gifted real estate agent was his disdain for failure. He hated it. And when he did fail he'd often beat himself up for days at a time. It was always Sara who repaired his ego enough to bring him out of whatever funk he found himself in but this time she wasn't there because he'd failed them both.

Hanging his head in defeat, the words of the newspaper article seemed to leap off the page and all his unanswered questions returned to him. Jacob couldn't shake the feeling of familiarity toward the boy. His curiosity transformed into a near obsession. He had to know how that boy could be so talented and who he was. He couldn't pin point why it bothered him so much but all he knew was he needed answers.

Then the fog seemed to lift. He spotted something in the picture; a smile that lit up the boys face. Could it be? "No it can't be him!"

CHAPTER SEVENTEEN
Reflections

On a mission, Jacob got up, slipped on his boat shoes and headed down the hallway to where he'd last seen Alex. When he reached the end of the hall he turned left and followed the corridor to its end. There, he found a service elevator, its door already opened, seeming to invite him in. The plain metallic walls and the drab carpet on any other day would be unappealing to an outsider but not for Jacob, not today. He was determined to find Alex and get some answers.

He climbed in and pushed the button to go down to the 2nd floor hoping to find Alex there. He needed to know if he was the 'symphonic prodigy' depicted in the newspaper or if he had slipped into a sleep deprived madness. The elevator screeched and groaned in its descent. A random thought pushed its way into his mind: *Why do you care?* which gave him pause. "Why *do* I care?" he repeated out loud. But his common sense quickly gave way to his compulsion for answers. He continued the pursuit motivated by his need to know.

When the door opened he stepped out and headed toward the hallway, studying it for several minutes to ensure he wouldn't miss Alex coming out of one of the guest rooms but there was nothing. Strangely, it seemed like there was no one anywhere just the faint glow of the hallway lights. "Strange" he said. But he knew that finding Alex would be the answer to all of his questions. He returned to the elevator to repeat the process one floor down but came up with the exact same result, nothing... not a sole. *What am I the only guest in this place?*

When he returned to the elevator there was one button left, outlined in with a vibrant green square: **B**. He guessed it led to the basement but *he* couldn't imagine Alex hanging out down there. He hesitated for several moments, calculating the worth of his mission. Still... driven by his insatiable curiosity, he pushed down the button.

The elevator door squawked as it closed and then made another slow descent. When he reached the bottom the elevator lightly bobbed up and down a couple of times finally settling in before opening the doors.

He stepped out of the elevator to a short corridor, the elevator doors closing quickly behind him. The air was stale and the entryway dimly lit. "Man, is this place creepy or what?" he said out loud to himself before turning to escape back the way he came. He pushed the button to recall the elevator but the button didn't light. He pushed it several more times before he heard the elevator's familiar popping sound echoing in its shaft. The formerly unsettling sound was now transformed to the sound of salvation which eased his mind.

When the sounds of the elevator suddenly went silent and the doors didn't open, his heart beat just a little faster. He frantically pushed the button several more times but nothing happened. His mind flashed to every horror movie he'd ever seen, making his palms sweat and his breathing grow a little more rapid. He felt like a caged animal. *Fight or flight.* He took a few deep breaths, slowly talking himself through the situation to try and easy his rattled nerves, "Okay, just calm down. You're fine. You're just going to have to find another way out of here."

"Hello!" he called out into the darkness. He waited a beat before hearing only his echo in response. "Hello, is anyone down there?" he said, taking a few steps away from the elevator. The entryway ended abruptly before he could see the long hallway to his right, a soft white glow in the distance was the only light visible.

He took one last glance at the elevator and then back down the hallway before he took one hesitant step, then two down the long, dark corridor. He walked slowly at first but his overactive imagination created boogiemen waiting for him in the shadows. As the hair on the back of his neck continued to stand, his pace quickened.

"A door. Thank God!" he said as his apparent destination came into view. He suddenly stopped because what he saw was nothing short of awe inspiring. "Remarkable!"
he whispered, examining a pair of beautifully hand carved wooden doors. They were much larger than typical doors. Jacob was no expert but they appeared to be made of an expensive cherry oak that had polished brass plates which met in middle. One door, the one on his right, had faces of children carved with a sculptor's skill. It looked so real. Each of the carvings was slightly different from the next. Some looked young, even infantile and others were older. Something stirred inside of him, that familiar feeling he'd had when he met Alex. There was something about the face, maybe the set of the eyes that made him feel a connection with them. *But why?* he thought marveling at the carving in the middle.

He noticed the door on his left was identical in every way except one. *Are these the same faces?* he thought as he closely examined them. The faces were there but incomplete. It was as if the sculptor was forced to stop before he'd finished his masterpiece. *Why wouldn't they finish their work?* Jacob wondered as he ran his fingers across one of the blank faces. A sudden sense of panic overwhelmed him and feelings of guilt, pain and deep regret burst out of his chest. Flashes of children leaped into his vision, their smiling faces abruptly vanishing right before him and their empty beings rushed him before they faded away into the darkness.

"Get away from me!" he screamed as the tears he'd desperately held back before now came forth and flowed freely down his face. The intensity of his emotions now completely consumed him. He threw open the faceless door trying to get away, stumbling then falling onto a hardened surface.

His strength was sapped and he laid there weeping, the pain agonizing. His mind battled against his emotions "What's happening to me?" he moaned as he laid there trying to reconcile his experience with reality. A profound sorrow replaced his confusion. In the deep silence, he finally recaptured his composure opening his eyes.

Jacob's attention was drawn to an amber light which now shown from the front of the room. He struggled to stand up, rubbing his eyes to clear his vision. He gazed across the room to see rows of seats all formed perfectly in rows and slightly curved to face a large stage. The perfect circle of light now focused on the center of the stage where a pearl white grand piano, its lid propped open to reveal is inner workings and amplify its sound, now sat abandoned.

"Maybe there's a backstage exit" he said as he walked slowly toward the stage keeping himself steady with the backs of the aisle seats. But by the time he'd reached the front row he'd regained some strength and was walking toward the stage on his own. He studied the stage and particularly the curtains trying to glean a pathway to the backstage and hopefully a way out of the theater and back to the hotel.

A mirror? he thought as the image of it came into view just behind the piano's bench. "That's strange…" he said as he made his way up to the stage. The mirror being so out of place intrigued him immensely. It was calling him, daring him to peer into its reflection so as to reveal its secrets. He walked toward it when, in its reflection, something caught his eye.

A little boy not much older than two years old sat looking at him through the mirror's reflection. Jacob was so taken aback by the toddler's presence he instantly froze. He couldn't see the boy directly just his image in the mirror. He watched the boy carefully, studying him and every move he made. He took a few more steps toward the mirror for a better look.

The closer he got to the mirror the more recognizable the boy seemed to him. "I know you, don't I?" he whispered trying not to startle the child. He reached into his memories trying searching for clues about when and where he may have met the boy, who he was, but he couldn't seem to place him.

Jacob took several more steps when the secret to the boy's possible identity started to become clearer. Images of him as a little boy, not memories of events but pictures he'd seen of himself as a child. Befuddled by the revelation Jacob said "Are you my..." The boy suddenly stood up but his reflection had suddenly and dramatically changed. His face had blurred out of focus. Jacob rubbed his eyes thinking he was seeing things and when he looked up the boy was gone. He hurried toward the curtain where he thought the boy was playing. "Little boy," he called out as he pulled the curtain to find him "where'd you go?"

Jacob searched everywhere he could but the boy was nowhere to be found. *There's no way he could've disappeared, he's not tall enough or old enough to have pushed past the doors of the theater* he thought.

Jacob returned to the mirror and examined it closely. The mirror was a tall one perfectly balanced on hinges with a wheeled base. The wheels had been locked into place so that the angle of the mirror could be adjusted. Jacob assumed it was for the performers of the theater.

He put his hand at the top and lightly pushed it forward. A woman came into its view at the very edge of the theater atop of the cat walk that encircled the theater's inner walls and led to the spotlights situated high above the audience. He tried to make out more than her silhouette when the horror of what he was seeing became evident to him. She was dangling a boy over the edge. He instantly knew it was the boy he'd just seen but before he could spin around to call out, the woman lost her grip on him and gravity's hand reach up from the floor and pulled the boy earthward.

Jacob instinctively closed his eyes to shield himself from seeing the tragedy which was about to unfold when he heard a loud "snap" cut through the air erasing any trace of the light in the room or the heartbreaking scene he'd just been witness to. "Someone help!" he cried out his eyes still not adjusted to the darkened theater.

"Someone, anyone please turn the lights back on a boy needs help, he's been hurt!" he shouted more forcefully now as panic started consume him. Pain shot down his spine as he felt the room spinning and collapsed to the floor, the blackened room now invaded and overtook him. Images of the woman and boy faded into its grip until there was nothing left but the darkness.

CHAPTER EIGHTEEN

Images Of Downs

She was painfully aware of the emptiness of the room as she woke. The unfamiliar view of waking up on Jacob's side of the bed came into focus though she knew where she was. *I must've taken up the whole bed last night* she thought. She pulled the pillow up to her face and took in a deep breath to immerse herself in his smell. *I miss him so much, I wish he'd come home* she thought.

She loved Jacob. They were soul mates… at least *she* always believed they were. But now, she just wasn't sure of anything anymore, except that he hadn't come home. It was something he'd never done before which was starting to concern her. They'd had their share of fights where one or the other would leave for a few hours but never all night.

Maybe I should call him she thought. She picked up

her phone and dialed the number. It rang several times before his recorded greeting started to play. She waited for the beep "Hey, you didn't come home last night. Um... well, just call me back" she said then hung up.

Maybe his cell phone is acting up again she thought. It wasn't uncommon when Jacob was on business trips for him to be in a place where his cell phone struggled to get a signal and they'd have to communicate by text. "Just checking on you, text me" she said as she typed and then pressed send.

On her nightstand was the 4D picture of their son. She didn't remember bringing it back from the kitchen but she shrugged, guessing she had just forgotten in all of the commotion. She sat for several moments studying the picture. She closed her eyes to imagine what her son might look like when she held him for the first time. Images came and then faded before coming into full focus.

It was nearing an hour since she'd sent the text to Jacob. She looked at her phone to see if she had missed a notification that he'd replied to her but he hadn't. She dialed his number again and again it went to voice mail "I was just calling to see if you were okay. I guess you don't want to talk. I understand. Take all the time you need" she said slightly irritated. She hung up and took a deep breath to shake off her frustration.

She held up the 4D picture again to study it trying again to picture her son in her arms. She'd never had a reason to study the subject of Down syndrome but she did now. And now her curiosity was driving her. She pulled out her smartphone and did an image search for babies with Down syndrome. Soon the screen filled with faces of babies. She enlarged the first one to fit on her screen and studied the baby's face carefully. Then she looked back to her son's picture and then back to her phone. She moved on to the next baby's picture and then the next repeating the process.

Before she knew it, an image of her son began to form. His eyes bright and warm tapering off at the edge like little brown almonds, while his tongue hung just outside his lips and his smile... his smile filled the entirety of his face, which would fill her heart with joy each time he smiled. His little ears folded at their tips hung perfectly in their place.

She began to relax as a peaceful calm returned to her. She looked up to see a single ray of sunlight piercing the darkened clouds just outside her window. It was symbolic of how she felt now. The gloom of the diagnosis had hidden her usually bright personality but now a single ray of hope seemed to penetrate her sadness. It was clear to her now that a perfectly woven human being stirred inside of her. It was a picture only God could have created.

She glanced at the time. It had been over an hour since leaving her last message to Jacob adding to the whisper of a doubt already lingering in her mind. Did he really care about her or their son? She certainly hoped so, because she knew when she told him to leave she had hurt him. How badly? She wasn't sure but she couldn't shake the guilt she felt over it.

Despite it all, as she looked over the horizon that was painted in varying shades of oranges and blues. Something warm kindled inside of her, a soft voice that wasn't her own kindly answered, *I do care about you and your son.* A smile drew itself onto her face and she knew. She knew in that moment that there was nothing in the depths of heaven or hell or earth that would keep her from loving her son.

She turned to a picture of her and Jacob on the nightstand, "I wish you knew how special your son was and I hope someday you will see it for yourself. I will *never* give him away! I don't care how hard this is or how different he is. I'll take care of him, even if I have to do it alone" she said as tears streamed down her face. She was happy and alive. And for the first time in a long time, she was confident in her decision. She might have sounded crazy to anyone listening to her but she didn't care.

Her spirits lifted and with her mind now reinvigorated she had the desire to shower and get dressed up for the day ahead. She hurried into the master bathroom and turned on the shower to warm the water.

She looked at herself in the mirror "Who are you?" she asked her reflection as she fiddled with her hair, which looked like a birds nest. "If I'd let it go any longer I may have had to shave it all off," she laughed, imagining herself bald "No... I don't do bald." She closely examined her other self in the mirror trying to find any other flaws she would need to address.

Noticing the steam barreling out of the shower she shed her remaining clothes and stepped into the water. The hot beads of water felt like heaven against her back. She tipped her head back allowing the warmth of the water to wash over her. She stayed in the shower until the water went cold, forcing her out.

She reached for the towel and wrapped her hair before reaching for a second towel when the bump in her abdomen caught her eye in the mirror. She stood in front of it admiring her belly before turning to the side to gaze at it from a different angle. She imagined her son nestled comfortably inside. A smile took control of her face. Looking at her stomach she said firmly "That's my baby boy in there," then looking down at the top of her belly said "And I love you, do you hear me? I love you!"

CHAPTER NINETEEN

True Friends

The long shower washed away many things, with every cleansing stream of water the remaining grief had been washed away. She brushed her hair absently humming the tune to Open Arms by Journey. It was her and Jacob's song. She remembered the first time he ever sang it to her; it was their first date. He had taken her to a karaoke club, his face flush with nerves as he stood eyes fixed on her with microphone in hand he sang Open Arms by Journey to her. From then on that had been their song.

Jacob didn't know it but Sara took it as a sign that he was the one. She'd grown up hearing her dad play oldies but Journey was his favorite and she had learned every word. *Open Arms* held a special memory for her because her dad would sing it to her

126

mom most days as long as she could remember. "Dad, you sound *terrible*," she used to complain. He'd simply reply, "Love sounds good in every key." It wasn't until years later that she understood what her dad meant.

After a few moments of blissful recollection, she got dressed. She felt herself coming back to normal. No, better than normal. She put her shoulders back as she looked at herself in her vanity table mirror. The woman she saw was barely recognizable compared to the shell of herself she'd been lately. Although her face was slightly skinnier and her eyes were a little bloodshot, her cheeks were vibrant with color and her smile bright with life. "This is me," she told herself sternly. She was confident about the direction of her life for the first time since the diagnosis.

After a few moments of self examination and reliving the good old days she focused on the day ahead. "Today, I take my life back" she announced. *I know, I'll go shopping for clothes for my baby boy* she thought looking at her belly before starting to put on her makeup.

Being the perfectionist that she was, she started to apply her make up with laser focus. It was funny how a little make up could make her feel put together. Jacob had always complained about how long she was taking to get ready, asserting that she didn't need any help being beautiful but she was always more critical of herself than anyone else could be, she loved that about him. She was applying her blush when the doorbell rang catching her by surprise. With the brush in hand she headed downstairs. A big part of her hoping it was Jacob. It seemed unlikely, *after all, why would Jacob ring the doorbell* she thought. Still... she hoped it was him.

She peered through the peephole of the door to find her best friend Stacey standing in the doorway, arms folded. Her heart dropped, she didn't look very happy... Sara remembered her phone ringing several times and Stacey nearly beating their door down and how she'd just ignored it. She opened the door "Stacey... what're you doing here? I mean - how are you?"

"Why haven't you called me back?" She demanded, scowling at her. She was tall, her legs long and athletic. Her typically dark, free-flowing hair was pulled into a messy ball at the top of her head. Sara was familiar with that look of disappointment and frustration. Stacey was sturdy, independent and very opinionated.

"Um..." she said unable to find adequate words, "so good to see you?"

"What's going on with you?" Stacey interrupted. "It's not like you to wait this long to call me back. I was starting to worry about you when you didn't call me back! Did I do something wrong? Do I need to beat somebody up? Talk to me!"

Sara held up her hand avoiding her gaze, searching for the right words to say. She began slowly, "I'm... I'm sorry I didn't call you. *You* didn't do anything." Stacey studied her face closely, looking for any sign of deception. Sara was bad at confrontation, and she would rarely tell Stacey that she did something wrong until it was long after the fact. Sara took a step back, letting the door swing wide behind her, silently inviting Stacey in.

"Well? Are you going to tell me what's been going on?" She said it in a way that didn't reflect a question. It was more like a demand and anyone who didn't know Stacey might have been offended by her candor. Being friends since they were kids, Sara didn't think twice about it. She knew it was only a reflection of her concern. They were polar opposites. Stacey was sporty, energetic and loud, full of confidence, while Sara was mild mannered and quiet unless you pushed her too far. Sara was as capable of raising hell just like Stacey was but it took her longer to get there.

Sara was still fighting to find the right words to present her situation to Stacey. She had never been good at delivering difficult news either. Stacey gave her a withering look. Sara offered her a seat, which she eagerly took, clearly unnerved by her friends secrecy.

"So how've you been?" Sara said awkwardly, filling the silence as she sat down.

"Don't do that!"

"Do what?" She said trying her best to look confused.

Stacey glared at her. "You're avoiding the question." she insisted.

"Well... um." Sara paused again for what seemed to be the hundredth time; conflicted, she fiddled with her fingers.

"I thought we were best friends," Stacey reminded her. "Just tell me! Whatever it is you know you can talk to me." When that didn't get the reaction she expected she probed. "Is Jacob cheating on you?" She asked but then immediately, "Oh my God! He is, isn't he? WHEN I SEE HIM HE'S GONNA..."

"Whoa, whoa wait a minute!" Sara quickly amended, "Jacob's not cheating on me. It's nothing like that... he... he just left."

"HE LEFT! What do you mean he *just left*?" She shouted forcing the chair backwards, making it cry out against the stone floor. One hand forming a ball she continued, "Where is he? I want to talk to him!"

Stacey's face had burned bright red. She had always been a protector. As the oldest of six siblings, she made it her job to take care of the people she loved. This wouldn't have been the first time

Stacey had protected Sara from dirt bags. Jacob wasn't a dirt bag though, although she might have trouble convincing her of that. "Stacey calm down. I told him to leave."

"What? Why?" She said stunned, pulling herself back towards the table even more attentive than before.

"It's complicated." Sara said evasively, looking away again.

"It's not complicated and I'm not leaving until you tell me what on earth is going on here!" She sharpened her stare at Sara. If there was one thing Stacey was good at, it was getting answers. She was unrelenting in her pursuit, and it was part of what made her a good friend for Sara. Whenever she sensed something was wrong they had a long talk until Sara finally told her what was going on. Today would be no different and Sara knew it.

"Fine but this has to stay between you and me... I don't want anyone else to know" Sara said.

"Of course I won't say anything" she rolled her eyes but laid an empathetic hand on Sara's.

"A couple of weeks ago we had an ultrasound and found out we were having a boy..."

"That's great news! But... go on" Stacey prompted, unwilling to wait for her to work through another bout of silence.

"Anyway, a few days later the doctor called us into

a meeting and told us that our son has Down syndrome."

"Down syndrome?" Stacey interrupted, her expression softening as she realized the gravity of the situation.

"It's hard to explain... I don't know all the details yet" Sara explained. "All I know is that he has an extra 21st chromosome. I know it means there will be some delays in his speech and learning, and then... well, there's a possibility that he could have several, more serious medical problems." By the last word Sara's eyes were misty.

"Like what type of problems?" Stacey asked her face growing more and more concerned. She squeezed Sara's hand in comfort.

"Like," she let out a long, heavy sigh, "like seizures, heart problems... Leukemia..."

Stacey let the words hang in the air for a moment before she responded, "I know you probably don't want to hear this... but you really have to trust God's plan on this one. He wouldn't give you more than you could handle."

"Jacob wants to end this pregnancy and try again in a few months" Sara sighed.

"Oh" she said calmly, "that's why you told him to leave, isn't it?"

Sara nodded as the tears welled up in her eyes. She grabbed a tissue and blotted her face just below her eyes trying desperately to save the hour she'd spent putting on her makeup.

"And you don't want to end it?" She asked.

"Of course not. You know I can't. It goes against everything I believe in. I saw his heart beating for goodness sake! I didn't just hear it and I didn't imagine it. I saw it with my own two eyes. How could he even ask me to consider that?" she said, returning to her resolve. "I'll raise my son on my own if I have to. If that's what it takes I'll do it. I'll give him the best life I can. I just can't let him go... I can't. I don't care what other medical problems he *might* have! All I know is that no matter what they say or how long or short his life is; I just want him to know he's loved... and wanted."

After her impassioned speech, Sara finally noticed that Stacey was sitting with her hand raised like she was a schoolgirl, waiting for her teacher to acknowledge her. She put her hand down and said "Before I start, I need you to know I'm on your side. I'll always be on *your* side. We've been through everything together. I'm here for you but let me play devil's advocate for a second. If you knew your baby would suffer and then die anyway, why wouldn't you consider ending it before it starts?"

"Why wouldn't I?" she hesitated in reflection. A phrase resounded in her head, still and small: *that the works of God might be revealed in him.* She smiled to herself, knowing her answer. "Because... God wants to use him." As Sara's own words settled in the air and in her heart, they became as real as Stacey. God had a plan for her son and deep down she knew it was an important one.

"Exactly! He has a plan for your son and it doesn't matter how big or small that plan might be - it's *his* destiny." Stacey said.

It had been too long since Stacey and Sara had spent any real time together. Life had caught up with them, keeping them from hanging out the way they usually had done. It was refreshing to Sara, who had spent the better part of her day with Stacey, with a pint of double fudge ice cream and her feet propped up on Stacey's lap. There were many tears, some laughter and some bursts of outrage and Stacey was there through all her ups and down the whole day. They were winding down from their day together over a light dinner Stacey had thrown together from what Sara had left in her fridge.

"When did you learn to cook?" Sara asked playfully. "The last time you tried to cook something, you had to replace the carpet because the smell of whatever you'd burned wouldn't come out."

"YouTube," Stacey said, deadpan. "You can learn to do anything on YouTube."

"Yeah, well, I wish they had someone on YouTube who could answer my questions."

"What questions?" Stacey pushed away the plate in front of her, giving Sara her full attention.

"To start with, why I've been having the same feelings I had when I lost mom. I mean, my son is here growing inside me," she said rubbing her belly "but the way I've felt you'd thought I'd lost him or something. And then I feel guilty for feeling that way. I know... it's confusing but that's why I was avoiding everyone" Sara shrugged her shoulders.

"Well, that's not fair to you. You're acting like this isn't major and you're just throwing a tantrum because your son's going to look a little different than you expected. It's not *like* that. When you found out you were pregnant, didn't you imagine your baby to be healthy? Perfect in every way?" By now Stacey was making large gestures with her hands, as if her hands were emphasizing her words somehow.

"Yes, of course," Sara replied. She sensed that these questions were leading her to a certain point that Stacey wanted to make, which was typical of her. It was a quality Sara appreciated but hated at the same time.

"Finding out your baby has Down Syndrome is *not* some conflict of preferences. It's not like you're asking for blonde hair and getting brown. This is you believing that your baby was healthy this entire pregnancy but finding out that might not be the case. Don't you think that shattered that image of the

perfect baby you'd built up in your head?" Stacey
continued, growing more and more passionate.

"I guess, yeah," Sara said.

"You fell in love with the baby you imagined but
that dream; that perfect, undiagnosed baby... well,
that baby doesn't exist anymore. In so many ways,
the dream you had for your life... your son's life
died. Does that make sense?"

"I never thought of it like that. But ever since the
diagnosis I was grieving like he *had* died. It confused
me because I knew he wasn't' dead, I saw his
heartbeat. I knew I shouldn't have felt that way but I
couldn't help it."

"Stop saying 'I shouldn't have felt this way or that.'
It doesn't matter what you 'should have' felt. The fact
is you *did* feel that way. You were grieving the loss of
the child that you dreamed would be in your life.
Give yourself some grace. This obviously hasn't been
an easy journey for you. Now, you just need to fall in
love with your son all over again. The one you're
going to have." Stacey said gently.

"That's the thing, I already have" Sara paused
looking at directly into Stacey's eyes. It was silent for
a few moments before Sara said "Thank you for
being such a great friend."

"You don't have to thank me! I'm here for you,
that's my job as your best friend. I just wish you
hadn't waited so long to talk to me about this. I

forgive you though." She winked at her, nudging her with her elbow.

"I know that, I'm just grateful. You really showed up at the perfect time. You always know how to explain things in a way that makes me feel better."

"Well, you're welcome," Stacey said with a beaming smile. "You look tired, love. I think I should go so you can get some rest."

" No! You don't have to leave..." she said, although her eyes were still a little puffy from crying and lack of rest.

"Oh no, I insist that you go straight to bed. I'll clean up here and then let myself out."

"Stacey I can't let you do..."

"Nope! Get to bed!" Stacey cut her off. She gave her a look that reminded her more of a mother than a best friend.

Sara put her hands up in submission and quietly turned and headed toward the stairs "Okay... you win. I'm going..."

"Good."

"I love you!" Sara shouted back at the base of the stairs.

"I love you, too!"

CHAPTER TWENTY

Nightmares

"Help me! Someone help me!" Jacob's words came out muffled in his ears but he was sure he was screaming. The nightmare was still lingering in his consciousness. After a long moment, he began to recognize his hotel room and with relief he remarked to himself, "Oh thank God! It's just another bad dream." He put a hand over his heart, it drummed rapidly against his palm. Taking several deep breaths he tried in vain to calm himself. *What's the deal with all these nightmares?* He wondered.

He sat back down trying to focus on anything other than what he had just dreamt but the vividness of the dream wouldn't leave him. His head throbbed and his hands shook as he recounted the experience, still seeing and feeling every detail. He stared out the window of his room and although the moonlight's glow painted the night sky, all he could see was the woman losing her grip and the boy falling. He had never had a dream that left that kind of unshakable impression before.

An hour passed, then two. In the distance, dawn was once again was on the march toward a new but repeated victory over its nighttime adversary. The heaviness of the previous night was being peeled away by the bright, warm rays that slowly but surely overtook his room. "Why is this place so bright?" he complained as he held up his hand to shield his eyes but it didn't help. The light pierced his head like a sharp knife, every beam of light hitting him directly in the eyes. He squinted hard against them, trying to resist their power. He retreated to the bathroom and closed the door. The light skillfully worked its way into the darkened sanctuary from under the door, lighting up the room.

Just as before, the morning's radiance dimmed to a soft glow leaving Jacob standing in the now barely lit bathroom. While the room darkened he let his mind wander briefly to the unusually bright lights. He tried to rationalize why they were so bright but couldn't find an explanation that made sense and everything in Jacob's world had to make sense. So he pondered the impossibilities to piece the unexplainable puzzle together but he was left with no truly acceptable answers. He didn't put a lot of credibility in angels and demons but he couldn't help but allow the thought of some sort of supernatural explanation to provide a possible rationalization.

Yeah, maybe an angel was in my room and couldn't find me, then left he thought sarcastically as he reached over to the light switch, flicking it on. He looked at himself in mirror which sent his imagination back to the theater. The endless movie replayed again and again as he saw the boy falling; something he wished he'd never seen and wanted desperately to forget. He closed and opened his eyes, focusing only on his reflection. He didn't recognize the man he saw looking back at him. His hair was a mess, seemingly lighter than his usual color, his eyes were swollen and bloodshot. "Man, I look like…"

His self examination was interrupted by the soft tapping echoing through his room. Jacob cautiously opened the bathroom door half expecting someone or something to burst out of the closet but to his relief there was nothing there. The tapping continued and he recognized that it *was* someone. And whoever it was, was knocking on the door. He flung the door open and found Alex standing there, holding out the paper. He inhaled deeply, took the paper and asked, "How much do I owe you?"

"Nothing, it's a present. Like the ones you get on your birthday," Alex replied a smile brightening his face.

Jacob couldn't help being drawn in by Alex's smile. His smile used every part of his face, his mouth was partially open and stretched from ear to ear. His eyes lit up with the excitement of a boy on Christmas morning. Even his forehead wrinkled in a way that screamed "I'm happy!" It seemed so odd but at the same time, inviting. It raised Jacob's spirits, which confused him, "Why are you so happy?" he asked having temporarily forgotten his previous night's events.

"I don't know, I was born that way."

Seeing that the direct approach wasn't going anywhere "Okay then, what else were you born with?" Jacob asked quizzically.

Alex looked at him puzzled by the question. He shrugged his shoulders and said "Just Alex parts" then turned and started down the hallway. Jacob was thrown by his response and stood there with a dumb look on his face.

His memory of the blurred face of the boy from his dream occupied him for a moment. When he snapped back into the present moment, he realized Alex had left. "Alex wait!" he called out. Jacob wanted to asked him about the boy in the paper from the day before but Alex had already rounded the corner and disappeared.

He started down the hallway after Alex but immediately recalling what had happened the last time he tried to find Alex, he stopped before taking a second step "Oh no, I'm not up for another chase today" he chided himself.

He went back into his room, tossing the paper on the table. He took a step over to the nightstand to retrieve the hotel's notepad and pen. The drawer was old and protested in agony when Jacob pulled at its ancient slides. His eyes immediately found the Bible hidden inside and was compelled to open it. He pulled it out, brushing a thin layer of dust from the cover and started to flip through the pages. He began reading half heartedly, daring God to speak through one of the passages. He stopped randomly on a page that read in big bold letters: JOHN. He thumbed through until he felt comfortable, "Chapter nine is as good a place to read as any," he mumbled to himself

"As Jesus was walking along, he saw a man who had been blind from birth," Jacob read aloud "Rabbi," his disciples asked him, "why was this man born blind? Was it because of his own sins or his parents' sins?" Jacob looked up, confused. *How could his parents doing something stupid even make him blind? he* challenged. Just as he was about to give up and close the book on this whole "God" thing, the red text seemed to jump out at him. Although he'd never read the Bible in its entirety he knew enough about the Bible to know that red text meant that Jesus was talking. "It was not because of his sins or his parents' sins, Jesus answered. This happened so the power of God could be seen in him."

Questions swirled in his mind. frustrated and perplexed, Jacob slammed the Bible closed and tossed it back into the nightstand. "What does that even mean? The power of God could be seen in him... Bah, how is God going to do anything with a kid that has..." he didn't see the point of even finishing the statement. His heart hardened "Why did I expect to find some kind of answer in an outdated book that only makes you ask more questions than it answers?" He grabbed the pad and pen and slid the drawer shut, refusing to give it another thought.

Then closed his eyes and did his best to draw the face of the boy and the hand carved door at the entrance to the theater while it was fresh in his mind. He was no artist but he was a fairly descent doodler. When he'd finished he sat marveling at the image of the boy.

He glanced down at the table and saw the headline:

'Eugenic Abortion': With Pre-Natal Testing, 9 in 10 Down Syndrome Babies Aborted

Jacob skimmed the article but one sentence caught his attention. *"'Less than a decade later, with the widespread availability of pre-natal genetic testing, as many as 90 percent of women whose babies were prenatally diagnosed with the genetic condition chose to abort the child...* "Wow, I guess my doctor wasn't the only one giving his patients *options*" he said recalling the doctor's office visit and his own conversation with the doctor about *their* options.

And I guess I'm not the only one who doesn't want that life, he thought as he recounted the recent events that had led him to this hotel.

His attention was drawn back to the picture he'd sketched of the door. In particular, the door with blank faces. He could picture it perfectly in his mind as if he'd been transported back, standing once again in front of the door peering into the faceless children that had been etched into it. His mind racing with questions. "Why? I mean, what's the *purpose* of faceless children?"

He stared at the paper but all he could see was the boy in the mirror and his tragic end. He felt pangs of nausea and the throbbing under his forehead that indicated a panic attack. He had only experienced this kind of anxiety once before when he was younger.

He and his friends were hanging at a place called 'Goat's Bluff'. Jennie was there with some of her friends, her and Jacob were acquaintances but nothing more. She decided to try to climb down the face to another ledge just below where they were standing. She was free climbing when the rock she was holding broke free sending her tumbling to the ledge below and then over it. Jacob watched in horror as she simply disappeared.

Although he was able to climb down and rescue her, the experience had affected him deeply. Even after more than a decade he still couldn't look over the edge of any vertical face without his nerves being rattled. And now that same feeling had come back to seize him again. He pressed his eyes tighter and tighter together trying to ward off reliving the experience from his dream.

He directed his thoughts to Sara. Her perfect, heart shaped face when it blushed. It made his heart stop. The way that her dark brown hair fell in messy waves down her back and her light brown eyes lit up when he said just the right thing. Or how she looked at him like there was no one else in the entire world she could love more. *"Remember that time in Belize?"* he imagined asking her. *"Remember how blue that ocean was? The warm air? I promised that the best was coming and you said 'well, the best can come but if there's ever a worst, we're in this together.'"* There was a sense of peace that washed over him at the sound of her voice causing his anxieties about his dream to subside. The joy of the memory was quickly replaced by the feeling of nostalgia. *So much for being in this together,* he thought bitterly. He felt so drained by it all and once again he felt himself starting to nod off.

He tried to force himself awake, shaking his head to wave off the sleep that begun to creep in. Recognizing he was losing the battle, he stood up and attempted to step away from the table. His foot hooked its corner leg and he stumbled in slow motion. He made a valiant attempt at regaining his footing but he couldn't exactly compete with gravity. He watched as the ceiling passed by, the nightstand next to the bed came into view, the edge caught him squarely on the jaw. Sharp pain seared through the right side of his face before the spinning room pulled him into the waiting darkness.

CHAPTER TWENTY-ONE
Spiderman Bandaid

His face throbbed and his head thumped as he came to. He reached up to his face to find a sticky substance covered his mouth and neck. After having inspected the point on his jaw where his face had met the nightstand, he examined his hand to find blood. He pulled the neck of his shirt out to find it was soaked red as well. *I'd better get this checked out,* he thought unsteadily as he stepped into the bathroom.

It was as though he had stepped into an odd black and white movie where other than the contrasting achromatic colors, he could only make out the color red, which now covered a significant portion of the outline of his face. He marveled at himself in the mirror trying to focus. He rubbed his eyes painting one of them red with the mess adding to the strange painting that was his reflection. He pulled down a hand towel, wet it with soothing hot water and covered his face before he was able to see the damage the fall had caused. "That's going to leave a nasty mark," he told himself.

Jacob cleaned himself up before he fumbled his way through changing clothes, slipping on his shoes and stepping out into the hallway. He turned toward the elevator and was surprised by Alex standing just outside his door holding the daily newspaper in his hand. His lively smile once again filled his face but this time Jacob's attention was drawn to his hands. They were shorter and more plump than he had expected but it seemed to fit in with all his other subtle nuances.

"What happened to you?" Alex asked his smile instantly changing to concern.

"I fell and hit my mouth," Jacob replied wincing from the pain.

"Let me see."

"Well, I was headed down so I could get this looked at. You don't know where the hospital is around here do you?"

Alex seemed puzzled, his almond-shaped eyes questioning. "You're gonna go to hospital just to get a Band-Aid?"

"What do you mean?"

"The cut on your face! It's so small!" Alex laughed, pointing to his chin.

"It can't be! Look at all the blood." Jacob stepped back into his room and into the bathroom for a closer look. The cut just under his chin was a mere quarter inch and although it had created enough blood to look as if he'd been beaten by a mob, it only looked to be a minor cut now. He went back out into the hallway where Alex was waiting "I guess I do just need a Band-Aid. Does the hotel have any Band-Aids, Alex?"

"I know where they are but you have to get a Spiderman one, not the Hello Kitty one" Alex said with the innocence of a small boy while signaling him to follow.

"Okay, buddy."

Alex grabbed his hand and led him down the hallway, Jacob could feel a genuine sense of caring that emanated off of Alex. "You're nice to everyone aren't you?" Jacob asked.

"Yes I'm nice to everyone, everyone is special," he replied.

"Well, what if they're mean to you?" Jacob pressed.

"That's okay, it's because they're not happy." he said innocently.

"What about your dad, is he good to you?"

"Yes, I love my daddy very much. He helps me be the best Alex I can be" he said as he turned to the left and back toward the service elevator.

Jacob's inquiry was interrupted when the elevator came into view. It was exactly how Jacob remembered it from before. Alex stepped inside but Jacob stopped short. "We're not going to the basement, are we?" he asked as his heart rate picked up.

"No silly, the Band-aids aren't in the basement." he said chuckling.

"Whew, okay then" he said oddly relieved "so, where are we going?"

"To the nursery!" he said proudly, "You're funny, Mr. Jacob."

The elevator stopped on the first floor where they both got off. Jacob followed Alex as he turned left and walked down a long hallway to the very end. The hallway had drab decor from the late 80's. The dim lighting added to the out dated atmosphere giving Jacob a sense of being out of place. "The Band-aids are just above where the people change stinky diapers." He instructed as he pointed Jacob into the room.

"Stinky diapers? You mean the changing table?"

"Yeah, that's the one but you go get it. I'm not going in there 'cause I might wake the baby." Alex said.

"No problem, I'll get it." He stepped into the room which was lit by a small night light in the corner. A rocking chair sat lifeless just past the crib and across

it was a small bed where a blanket bulged off its
surface. He went to investigate further and could
make out a small boy sleeping. *I definitely don't want
to wake you up little buddy* he thought as visions of a
crying toddler sent a chill down his spine. He turned
gingerly to avoid making any noise.

The changing table sat up against the wall a few
feet away. He slowly went to it and opened a top
cabinet. *Okay there's the diapers and baby wipes.* He
carefully closed the cabinet and then opened another;
there was some kind of cream. *He* pulled it down to
look at it more closely. *Diaper rash cream, okay… not
helpful* he thought. He continued searching through a
few more items before he spotted the Band-aid
boxes. One Spiderman and one Hello Kitty just as
Alex has said.

There you are he thought while pulling out the
recommended Superhero Band-aid box then
stepping into the restroom. He flicked on the light
and affixed Spiderman to his chin. *Well, at least Alex
will like it* he thought. Before he could inspect his
work the cries of a small child filled the room. Jacob
hurried back into the room to try to pacify the child.
"It's okay buddy, go back to sleep" he whispered.
The boy sat up in his bed and held his arms out for
Jacob to pick him up. The boy acted as if he knew
Jacob. Without hesitation he picked the boy up and
he instantly laid his head on Jacob's shoulder, his

face turned away. He was still slightly whimpering
"It's okay, let's try rocking you back to sleep…"
Jacob said unsure of what to do.

Jacob slowly rocked with the boy's head on his
shoulder. He could tell the boy was comfortable with
him and he was comfortable with the boy. It
reminded him of why he was so excited to be having
a son. The closeness they would share and the bond
they would create gave Jacob a sense of purpose.
And he could feel that purpose now resting in his
arms.

As he sat there rocking, his thoughts wandered in
and out of the moment. Images of him and Sara at
the hospital holding their newborn son occupied his
mind. He could imagine himself the day after,
beaming with excitement as he walked into work
handing out cigars, too proud to care what anyone in
the room was thinking. As he sat there completely
lost in thought, the little boy shifted his weight so
that he was laying in the crook of Jacob's bent arm.

The glow of the lights from the bathroom
illuminated the boy's face. Jacob gasped as the reality
of who the boy was, struck him. It was Jacob but it
wasn't. "This can't be… you were just a reflection!"
he said emphatically. "And… and I saw you fall from
fifteen feet, in a dream!" he continued uncertain what
to believe. The lines between reality and his dreams
had suddenly blurred sending Jacob into a panic.

He stood up and frantically put the boy back in the bed and turned away from him. "Uh, I must be dreaming…" Then interrupting himself, he turned around to look at the boy again. The boy was still there unchanged. "I must've hit my head harder than I thought because I'm definitely seeing things."

He almost tripped over his feet again as hurried toward the door. When he looked up to find the handle the door was open and there was a mirror… the same mirror from his dream was guarding the exit, stopping him dead in his tracks. "What?" His breathing was suddenly labored, his heart dropped down into his stomach. "This is impossible… what? Am I trapped in this nightmare or something?" he asked but knew he wasn't going to get an answer from anyone there. "Wake up, Jacob!" he screamed, slapping himself hard on the face. He winced as he watched his face blushed red with a hand print. "Either this is real or I'm insane, one of the two!"

Alex stepped in front of the mirror just as Jacob was about to call out for him. Before Alex could say anything he asked: "What's that mirror doing there!?"

"I don't know, the men came. They left it there. You want me to find them?" Alex asked calmly.

Jacob took a deep breath trying to regain his composure. "Um… no… no, that's okay." he replied. *Holy crap, either that's one heck of a coincidence, or I'm seriously losing it!* he thought.

Alex interrupted Jacob's thoughts. "Can I show you something?"

"What do you want to show me?" he asked unsure if he could handle any more surprises.

"Something special!" Alex said "Please, can you come with me?"

"Alright Buddy, anything to get outta here."

Alex excited reached up, took his hand again and practically pulled him down the hallway.

CHAPTER TWENTY-TWO

Faces

Jacob pressed Alex as they reached the elevator once again "Hey buddy, where are you taking me?"

"The secret hallway."

"Where's the secret hallway?" he asked as flashes of the drab dark hallway and the door with no faces instantly came to mind.

Alex pushed the button to the elevator and the doors open and he walked in and said plainly "the basement."

Jacob pulled his hand away abruptly. "Uh… I don't really want to go to the basement buddy."

An intense sadness came over Alex's face and tears formed in his eyes, his head dropped down. "Whoa… hey buddy, don't be upset it's just…" he contemplated how to explain his reluctance but couldn't find the words. *The kid is going to be with you, don't be such a coward!* he thought. "Alright... alright I'll come with you," he said holding both his hands up in surrender to try to calm him. Alex wiped his eyes and as the door closed his smile quickly returned.

As the door opened to the basement Jacob couldn't believe his eyes. It was exactly the same hallway as the one in his dream. Alex grabbed his hand and pulled. Jacob followed obediently, not even checking the button to see if it worked, fearing that it wouldn't. A feeling of Deja Vu overwhelmed him. *I've been here before but that was a dream. Wasn't it?* Questions swirled his head. *How is possible to dream something and then have it be real?* He wondered but it was all so confusing.

Alex didn't utter a word, he just kept pulling him toward the soft glow at the end of the darkened walkway. Jacob kept squeezing his eyes closed sensing they had betrayed him. Each time he opened them, reality paralleled his memory.

When they reached the double doors Alex slipped through the door to the right, the one the craftsman had completed. Jacob was weary about touching either door. He was especially careful not to touch the other door, the one with faceless children that had invaded his emotions leaving them scarred.

He didn't know if he was overwhelmed by his surroundings, or if it was the knock on his chin but

the room started to spin as he continued to follow
Alex. He reached out to steady himself, grabbing
hold of one of the carved faces. The detail in his hand
painted a perfect picture in his mind of an infant's
face, masterfully sculpted. Warmth emanated from
the face in the door. He could feel it flow down his
arm until it saturated him entirely.

He closed his eyes in fear but instead he was met
with an unexplainable sense of joy; a longing he
didn't understand at first. It was the same feeling he
had for Sara but it wasn't for her. It was a feeling of
love... true love. But this love was for the children...
children he didn't know.

He could feel the very source of their lives pulsing
through him. He lost himself in the images that
flooded his mind of children playing, laughing and
jumping around. They were having fun the way all
kids do. The only difference was their almond
shaped eyes and the way they smiled.

As his hand slipped off the carving a halo of pasty
yellow lights accented the door. He glanced over at
the other door and noticed it remained stark and
lifeless. He returned his attention to the finished
door. Its glow was inviting and he could hear the
muffled sound of a lullaby being sung. The squeaks
of a rocking chair as it gently glided across
hardwood, underscored the tune. He carefully
pushed the door open using the brass plate to avoid

contact with the wood. The sound grew louder as well his curiosity. *Who is that?*

As the room came into focus, a woman sitting in a wooden rocking chair singing a lullaby came into view off in the distance. She looked to be holding what one could only assume was a baby swaddled in a light blue blanket. She was perched atop the theatrical stage next to the white grand piano. *That's strange,* Jacob thought. *Could that be the woman from my dreams?*

The entire scene looked to be out of place. Jacob's curiosity urged him to investigate. He stepped across the threshold of the door and slowly walked down the long aisle of the empty theater. The golden theater had dark red and black folded seats that filled the room and matched the carpet that lined the floor.

When he reached the stage, he gazed at the woman in the rocking chair. He felt himself getting lost in her angelic voice which seemed to call to him, "Come closer." He found a way onto the stage and moved in, trying to get a look at the woman and the child. But all he could see was the top of her head as she focused on the baby whose face was hidden in the swaddled blanket. He tried from several angles to get a look but he couldn't make out any detail from any of them. He walked carefully trying hard not to disturb her or the baby. "Hello" He called to her softly.

No response.

He called again a little louder but again there was no response. She just kept rocking, looking down at the baby. He quietly inched closer trying to get a better look and hoping she'd look up at him but she wouldn't.

He lifted his hand to touch her shoulder to get her attention, when the piano started playing behind him. He turned to find Alex sitting on its bench playing.

"Alex, where'd you run off to? And what are you doing?" he questioned.

"I'm here. I'm writing," he answered.

"Writing? Writing What?" Jacob asked slightly frustrated by the vague answer.

"My next piece of music" Alex said innocently as he continued to press down the keys of the piano.

Jacob listened for a while and was in awe of Alex's ability. "You're amazing buddy!"

Alex stopped playing for a moment and looked up at him confused. "Who's Buddy?"

"Well... you're Buddy."

"Why do you call me Buddy? My name is Alex."

"I'm sorry, Alex, I call my friends buddy." Jacob quickly amended, unsure whether or not he had hurt his feelings.

Alex smiled so big his entire face lit up "So, we're

friends?"

"Yeah, we're friends, if you want to be my friend."

"Okay buddy!" Alex replied excited by the idea. "Hey Buddy, will you come see me play at my next concert?"

"Of course I will. When is it?"

"It depends."

"Okay then, where will it be?" Jacob asked.

"Right here. This is the old theater. It has the big numbers on it 321."

Jacob replied "321 huh. Okay… I'll come see you play as soon as I can."

Alex jumped up from the piano and wrapped his arms around Jacob hugging him "Okay buddy," he said as he burst into a full laugh. Jacob, not sure how to react, cautiously hugged him back.

CHAPTER TWENTY-THREE

Letting Go

Still chuckling Alex returned to the piano and started playing his song again. But the sound that filled the theater was much more than a simple piano piece. It was music that had the power to evoke emotion from even the most callused listener. Even though he was the only one playing, the Symphonic sounds reverberated throughout the theater. Jacob could feel each note as Alex played. Mesmerized by the vision of Alex and the white grand piano. He easily conjured up visions of a full orchestra playing with him.

As he studied Alex, he found he was completely fascinated by him. *How could someone like him be playing, much less composing such complex masterpieces? It's just not possible, is it?* As he contemplated his questions Alex abruptly stopped playing and pointed to the mirror that was behind him.

"Why did you stop playing?"Jacob asked. But his curiosity drove him toward the mirror to investigate why Alex just sat there pointing at it. He walked to its face and peered into its reflection. It was the same one from his dream and from outside the nursery which should have surprised him but he was almost expecting it. The same little boy was huddled between the curtains playing alone exactly how Jacob had seen him before. "Alex, do you know who that boy is?" he asked pointing at the boy in the mirror.

"That's your pretend son, he's the one you want to play with!" Alex said.

"Why do you say he's my pretend son?" Jacob made a face to demonstrate his confusion. He couldn't decide what he meant, or how he felt about what he said.

"Because he's not real."

"But he looks just like me when I was a little boy" Jacob protested.

"I heard my daddy tell a man one time that before I was born he was sad." Alex paused and looked as if he was trying hard to remember the exact words his dad said, "because he... he, wanted a son that was like him when he was a little boy, just like you do. But instead he got me."

"Just like me? How's that? I don't have a son yet..." as soon as he'd uttered the words, he heard the distinct sounds of his son's heartbeat that he and Sara heard during their ultrasound. "Yeah, but..."

Alex interrupted him "He's the son you wish you had, like when you make a wish on your birthday but he's not real."

"Who told you that?"

"He did."

"He did?" Jacob asked shocked. "If he's not my son then... who is my son?"

Alex stood up and handed him the newspaper with the headline that read: **Boy With Down Syndrome Stuns World With Beethoven-esque Symphony.** He pointed at the boy from the article. "Him" he said with the brightest smile Jacob had ever seen. It not only filled Alex's face Jacob could feel it leap off. It reminded Jacob of the brightness of his hotel room and his suspicions of an Angel being its source. *Could it be? Alex... an Angel?* Jacob desperately tried to dismiss the thought.

"You're telling me that my son is the boy who wrote those incredible symphonies?" he asked with amazement until he realized "wait... wait a minute. My son isn't even born yet so, how could this be my son?"

Alex's radiant smile seemed to glow even brighter and his eyes spoke to him as if they'd pierced Jacob's thoughts "God showed me" he said firmly. As his words reached Jacob's ears an unbelievable certainty came over him. He knew what Alex was saying was true. "God said 'don't be afraid Jacob.' He said to 'let him go'" Alex said pointing toward the mirror. "He told me to tell you that" he said, then simply turned around and returned to playing the piano.

Jacob felt like he'd been hit with a Tsunami of emotions all at once. He replayed in his mind the excitement he shared with Sara when they found out they were having a son followed quickly by the fight that they'd had. A flash of Nurse Hall in her southern accent saying "The Lord knows what he's doin." Then Linda jogging and her song that was playing *God blessed me broken, my eyes look to heaven.* The doors with the faces and the woman letting go of the boy from the cat walk all raced through the highlight reel of his mind in an instant. It was suddenly all very clear to him.

A tear trailed down making a path on his cheek. It hung off his jaw for a moment before falling gently onto the floor. Jacob looked up through teary eyes to see the boy in the mirror but this time he knew that it was just a reflection of his own desire. The boy simply wasn't real. He was merely a subconscious attempt to conform Jacob's reality. Just a simple replica of the boy who Jacob wanted his son to be but it was just that... a fake. The revelation overwhelmed him "I'm so sorry but you're not my son," he said. His tears now flowed freely, one after another. "I have to say goodbye..." he said.

The boy in the mirror looked up at him and in his innocence waved good-bye in the way that toddlers do. Jacob waved back in reaction but in the act itself, all of his grief, the buried emotions over his son's diagnosis hit him squarely in the heart ripping it apart. He agonized as the reality of what he had to do became crystal clear.

He reached up and placed both hands on the mirror, took one last long look at the boy through gushing tears and pushed as hard as he could. With the wheels at its base had been locked in place, the mirror tipped straight back. He watched as the mirror began to fall in slow motion. And for one fleeting moment regret made his heart skip a beat. He cried out "NO!" as he reached out to catch mirror and the image of the boy it held. But it was too late. The mirror slammed into the floor. A loud KSHH burst out from it landed. The acoustics of the theater amplified the deafening sound of breaking glass as the mirror exploded into a million tiny fragments showering the stage with sparkling crystals of regret.

Jacob collapsed to his knees, glass digging into them, weeping uncontrollably. Without warning he became aware of a sensation he'd never experienced before. With every tear he left on that floor a drop of peace took its place. "Dear God what have I done?" he moaned "Please help me, I can't do this without you!" he continued to cry out desperately. The full weight of his plan to convince Sara to terminate the pregnancy bore down on him accompany by its guilt. It was a weight too heavy to bear. Exhausted, he put his head down on the stage. He stayed there quietly listening to Alex play until he'd exhausted every tear. But it was through that pain that what he had to do next became absolutely clear. *No matter what it takes, I will get my family back!*

CHAPTER TWENTY-FOUR

Destinies

Jacob slowly pushed himself off the floor. The final notes faded into the acoustics of the room until there was nothing left but silence and the pool of tears he'd left on the floor. Behind him Jacob heard footsteps rushing across the stage. He turned to investigate and the woman from the rocking chair now disappeared behind the stage left curtain carrying her baby. Without thinking he turned and pursued her, leaving Alex behind. He pushed back the stage curtain and caught a glimpse of her leg as if she'd disappeared into the wall. He rushed to where she'd been only to find an unseen corridor. He raced down the hallway to catch up to her but the woman had simply vanished. "Where did she go?" he wondered out loud, "She couldn't have just disappeared." Although with all he'd experienced he wasn't entirely sure that wasn't possible.

The glow of two lights shining down on a set of two separate doors with the familiar star of dressing rooms was all he could see as he scoured up and down the hall. She had to be in one of the dressing rooms. He walked carefully toward the door and knocked gently on the first "Hello, Ma'am I just want to talk to you," he said as he turned the knob, carefully opening the door.

A table with a large dressing mirror was pushed against the wall directly across the room. Large frosted white bulbs bordered its large, reflective face. Jacob reached for a switch on the wall and flicked it on. The soft white light shot across the room revealing all of its secrets. Costumes hung on a pole anchored to the wall and various brushes lined the dressing table. Jacob could only assume they were used for make-up. No doubt this room had seen its share of actors and actresses come and go.

He stood quietly for a moment hoping for some indication of where the woman had gone. The muffled whispers of the woman drifted into the room "I won't let your daddy hurt you!"

Jacob spun around searching for the direction of her voice but wasn't able to decipher where she was. He stopped and listened intently. *Where are you?* he thought.

"He just doesn't know how special you are," the

woman's voice continued.

He studied the room carefully. He looked to the left, then right but she wasn't there. And there was nowhere she could be hiding. He crouched down to peer under the table when he heard the door to the next room close.

He dashed out of the room just in time to see the woman running down the hall "Wait!" he called out to her "Please!" When she pushed through an exit door, a high pitched alarm sounded. Its single wailing tone pierced his ears and he felt the vibration deep in his chest. He covered his ears with his hands while he ran for the same door in pursuit.

When he stepped out, the intensity of the sun blinded him. He raised his arm desperately trying to block the sun so his eyes could adjust. When they finally did he was standing in the alley that ran alongside the hotel. The sun was high but the frigid air sent a chill down his spine. He hurried around to the front of the building before he entered back through the main entrance.

"Good grief its cold!" he announced as the door closed.

"Weatherman said it's gonna stay that way for a while," said an unseen voice from behind the counter. The innkeeper stood up "Oh, Mr. Michaels, how are you today?"

"Did you see a woman holding a baby come

through here?" Jacob asked still somewhat unnerved by all that he had experienced.

"No, no one like that came in today."

Jacob walked back to the entrance door examining the parking lot hoping to catch a glimpse of the woman but there was nothing more than a light breeze ruffling some bushes at the far end of the lot. "You know Alex?" he asked.

"Yeah, of course I know him. I'm his Father."

"Does he have Down syndrome?" Jacob asked plainly, the words escaping him before he anticipated their possible impact. "I'm sorry, I don't mean to be so blunt."

"It's alright friend. He does, why do you ask?"

Ignoring the question Jacob said "I don't mean this the way it's probably going to sound but how could he be so talented when he's, well..." Jacob paused hoping the innkeeper would understand what he was getting at but he just stood there patiently waiting for him to finish his thought. "...so different from normal kids?" As the words left his mouth he tipped his eyes downward in submission anticipating a justifiable angry response.

The innkeeper gently asked "Do you have a gift?"

"What do you mean?"

"A gift, something you're good at. You know, something that comes easy to you."

"Yeah, I'm good at a couple of things."

"Have you ever had any challenges in your life?"

"Of course, who hasn't?"

"Well, did you ever have to struggle at something while you were getting good at the things you're good at now?"

"So many I can't count them all." Jacob said embellishing.

"Then how is Alex different than you?"

"He has Down syndrome."

"Yes, he does and that's been his life's challenge. He's had to and continues to have to overcome some difficulties from it. But that's all Down syndrome is, one of life's many challenges."

"Yeah but it's a big challenge and it still doesn't answer my question..." Jacob retorted.

"Sadly, the world is full of people just like you. When they look at someone like Alex all they see is a disability which they perceive to be a disadvantage. They see the negative side of Down syndrome and what these kids can't do, instead of looking harder to see what they can do. The truth is a person is only disabled if they believe themselves to be."

"C'mon he can't do what other people can, right? Doesn't that make him disabled?"

"No" the innkeeper replied curtly. "He may not be able to do what other people can do but other people can't do what he can do. That's what makes us all unique. We all have some sort of disadvantage in life that we have to overcome so we can perform at our highest potential. God created each of us to be individuals with distinctive gifts and talents and he didn't make any two of us exactly alike. It's what makes everyone person special. And because God created us and we're all special, He-" he lifted his finger and pointed to heaven "-has a plan for every one of us. Let me put it a different way." he said.

"Shoot" Jacob replied now intrigued.

"Do you have things that you aren't able to do because you're not good at them?"

"Of course I do, doesn't everyone?"

"Exactly, now you're catching on."

"No, I don't think I am." Jacob replied.

The innkeeper continued, ignoring his statement "Well friend, I believe our challenges don't define us. They simply shape our character and lead us to find our unique gifts and talents. The character we build through those challenges helps us to fulfill our God given destiny. Have you ever heard of Tim Harris or Karrie Brown?"

"Can't say that I have..." Jacob replied.

"Mr. Michaels," The innkeeper said in a fatherly voice.

"Please call me Jacob, Mr. Michaels was my dad." Jacob interrupted.

"Tim Harris is a young man who, after he graduated High School and then College started his own restaurant in Albuquerque, New Mexico called Tim's Place. And I hear the food is great and the hugs are even better."

"Hugs? Why would they give out hugs at a restaurant?" Jacob asked puzzled.

"Don't you see? Tim was born with Down syndrome but he didn't let that stop him from fulfilling his God given destiny. It's kinda funny but it says on his restaurant sign that they are the world's friendliest restaurant and they serve breakfast, lunch and hugs."

"Really, he has Downs?"

"Really. But the world's friendliest restaurant was God's plan for him. Down syndrome didn't prevent him from it. It's what made Tim's Place.... Well, Tim's Place!"

"Okay..." Jacob replied unsure of what to say next.

The innkeeper seeing his mental struggle continued "I read a story the other day about a junior in High School named Karrie Brown who had a dream to be a professional model. Recently her dream came true."

"Let me guess she has Down syndrome too, right?"

"She does," he said "But if you want a different example, someone who doesn't have Down syndrome, how about Professor Stephen Hawking, ever heard of him?"

"I read about him. He's that physicist guy that everyone calls the smartest man in the world, right?"

"Yeah, that's the one. He was diagnosed with Lou Gehrig's disease when he was 21 years old confining him to a wheelchair for life. Some would say he's disabled because he's in that chair and he can't even talk! He has to communicate through a computer. But did that stop him from reaching his highest potential?"

"No," Jacob admitted. "So what you're saying is, he's not 'disabled' he just defines his purpose differently than 'typical people'."

"Now you're getting it! Although he doesn't believe in God or a God given destiny, I do! And the way I see it, he's just uniquely abled for what God created him to do." the innkeeper asserted.

Jacob nodded his head that he understood.

"Now... let me ask you. Don't you think Alex deserves a chance to fulfill God's plan and try to leave his mark on this world no matter how big or small that might be?"

"Of course he does, he's amazing!"

"Then doesn't every child deserve that same chance? Doesn't your son deserve that chance?"

"My son..." he paused "How'd you know about my son?" he asked shaking his head "never mind, as a matter of fact, I was going to the woman I saw in the theater, then I was coming to check out to go home to be with my family and my son... my son, who will be born with Down syndrome," the words hung in the air for some time inching their way into Jacob's heart. A smile burst onto his face. "I'm having a son and I can't wait to see his beautiful face!" he shouted.

He turned to leave and the woman holding the baby was standing directly in front of him. He was completely shocked by who was standing there. "Sara!?"

Without saying a word she lifted the baby slightly toward him. The blanket on one side slipped just enough to expose the baby's face. He leaned in for a closer look when the room abruptly began to spin. The walls of the room started to close on him as he tried desperately to focus on his son's face, hoping to catch just a glimpse. He shook his head trying to hold on but a ball of brilliant white light exploded from the baby's face robbing Jacob of his vision. He stood blinded for what felt like years before the all the light in the room was swallowed by the black hole.

Darkness.

CHAPTER TWENTY-FIVE

Destiny's Call

For the first time since she'd been told of her baby's diagnosis she followed her usual routine. She immediately went straight to her dresser and pulled out her favorite flannel pajamas and tossed them on the bed. Then she went to her vanity table to remove her makeup but as soon as she saw herself she said laughing "I look like a circus freak!" Her mascara had blackened her eyes and where her tears had run down her face, there were black streaks, she looked like a tattered mess.

She cleaned off all her makeup, rubbed lotion over her face, arms and legs. Then she brushed her hair before she put a detangler in it and braided it to prevent the matting she'd dealt with that morning. She pulled off the outfit she wore and slipped on the pajamas laying across her bed. Finally she tugged the corner of the covers back making a perfect triangle, slid her feet under the covers and snuggled peacefully beneath them.

The only thing missing in her routine that night was Jacob's typical corny remark "Hey OCD queen, are you done yet?" or something similar. She missed him terribly. Her thoughts drifted to Jacob, their son and her day with Stacey. The sunset gave way to the twilight before she embraced her exhaustion and fell into a deep sleep.

She woke to the repeated sound of her cell phone's ringer, she glanced up at the digital clock on Jacob's nightstand as she watched the 20 change to a 21. "Who'd be calling me at three in the morning?" she grumbled rolling over until the ringing stopped before she tried to recapture the dream she'd been engrossed in. The phone forced her to wake again "What in the world!" she demanded flinging the covers off of her, grabbing her phone off the dresser mentally preparing to give whoever was calling a stern piece of her mind.

She looked at the caller ID: *General Memorial Hospital.* She quickly answered it, "Hello".

"May I speak with Sara Michaels please?" a woman on the phone asked.

"Who is this?" Sara snapped back.

"My name is Nancy, I'm an ER nurse at Memorial General, is this Mrs. Michaels?" she asked gently.

"Yes, this is she." She could feel her nerves swelling in the pit of her stomach. The nurse was taking far too long to get to whatever point she was supposed to make.

"You were listed on Mr. Michaels' phone as his ICE contact." she said. Immediately, Sara's heart dropped.

"What happened? Is Jacob okay?" she said anxiously.

"I need to confirm some things with you before I can say. Who is Jacob Michaels to you?"

"He's my husband! Now please tell me, is he okay?"

"Please just confirm his date of birth and then I can answer your question." Nancy said gingerly.

"November 2nd, 1978! Now please tell me what happened."

"Your husband was in a car accident and he's in the ICU. It's very serious and we think it would be best if you could get here as soon as possible." Nancy explained. "He's been here for almost a week and undergone several surgeries."

"Oh my God!" she gasped as the recollection of her screaming at him to leave her alone flooded her thoughts. "Why are you just now calling me?" She demanded.

"Your husband's phone was the only thing he had on him when he came in and it had a pass code on it.

Until tonight before his last surgery we weren't able
to access it." Satisfied with her explanation
she leapt into action "I'll leave right now. Can you
please text me the address from Jacob's phone?" she
asked.

"I'm really not supposed to use patient's phones."
she replied.

"You have my permission to use his phone and I
need it. Text to me so I can pull it up on the GPS and
get to my husband! So please either send it from his
phone or yours but please send it!" Sara voice was
curt but pleading.

"Yes Ma'am, I'll do it..." The nurse reluctantly
agreed.

Sara rushed to change clothes and pack bags for
her and Jacob while she waited for the text. "He's
walking out of that hospital!" she said with an
uncharacteristic determination. She scooped
everything up and headed downstairs to the garage
to wait.

She pushed the button to open the garage door
pulled the car into the driveway and with another
push closed the garage door behind her. As she was
preparing to drive off her mind was reeling. She
pictured Jacob bandaged up and unrecognizable,
tubes and wires coming from every direction so that
she couldn't tell where the machines ended and he
began.

179

321 DOWN STREET

Before she could allow her mind to wander too far her phone buzzed and lit up. The message from Jacob's phone appeared with just an address, she tapped on it before selecting the appropriate buttons to pull it up on her phone's GPS then set it in the dashboard cradle. She pressed down on the accelerator so aggressively that the tires made a high pitched screech before regaining traction and propelling her down the road into the night.

CHAPTER TWENTY-SIX

Hesitations

The markings of the road were barely visible as Sara drove through the winding road. Forest blackened by the night sky was only visible by the two narrow beams of her sedan's headlights. She'd slowed down considerably because of the eeriness of the road conditions. Although that wasn't the cause of her concern, the thought of not making it to Jacob in time was. She kept pushing out her deepest fears by staying focused on the road ahead.

She rounded another of the hundreds of sharp curves she'd already seen on the drive up but now she noticed something was different about it. A soft amber glow was coming from the top of a long straight stretch of road. But it wasn't from early light of dawn but from street lights twinkling against the clouds.

She pushed the car a little harder to make up some distance and slowed at the top of the hill. A large white speed limit sign was the first thing to come into view which read *Speed Limit 35 MPH* followed by *Welcome to Mountain Fork population 11,321 established 1866* as she started into the city. She followed the blue triangle on her phone to Main St and made a left turn "There's the hospital!" she said.

A red emergency sign with white lettering was off to the right. An ambulance with lights flashing was pulled up to the door though she couldn't see anyone around it. A blue visitor parking sign caught her attention which she reacted to by yanking the wheel hard to the left and pulling into the parking lot. She examined the lot carefully as she slowed *I want to get as close to the door as possible* she thought "there we go!" she said as she came to a stop, put the car in park and jumped out.

Sara hurriedly entered the hospital into the emergency room and went directly to the reception desk. "Hi, one of your nurses, Nancy, called me about my husband." she said anxiously.

An expressionless middle aged man sat behind the desk staring at a screen. "What's your husband's name Ma'am?" he said without ever looking up.

"Jacob Michaels, I was told he's in ICU"

Glancing at her for a moment as if sizing her up he

said "Go down here." he said pointing to hallway on the other side of the reception area "Take the elevator up to the 7th floor". He then returned his attention to his computer screen and whatever he'd been mesmerized by before she'd interrupted.

She followed the man's instructions and rode the elevator to the 7th floor. When she arrived on the floor she checked in with the night nurse who directed her to ICU room 3. She walked intently but cautiously to the front door of Jacob's hospital room. She stopped short of his room for a long time trying to prepare herself for whatever horrific sight would lay just beyond its threshold or what she might say if she found Jacob awake.

The remanence of the fight they'd had still lingered with her. She was torn between her love for him and her instinct to protect her child. But today she knew she had to set all of that aside and care for her husband. It made her oddly nervous.

"Mrs. Michaels?" A familiar voice asked from behind her. She nodded acknowledging she was her. "I'm Nancy, the nurse that called you earlier. I'm glad you were able to get here so quickly."

Nancy's words had caught Sara off guard but brought her back to the present after being lost in the depths of her thoughts "Please, call me Sara."

"No problem Sara. Have you been in yet?"

"No, I just got here."

"Why don't you go in and see Mr. Michaels, we can talk afterward."

"Is Jacob" she hesitated unable to form the words to finish her question. But the devastation at the thought of losing him was evident by the expression on her face.

"The doctor's say he's doing well considering and he should recover but more importantly, ever since he's been here, every time he wakes up he tells us he has something to tell you... that-" she stopped mid-sentence considering whether or not to continue.

Sara reached out and placed her hand on Nancy's shoulder and peered into her eyes "Please, you have to tell me what he said."

"Now we're not sure if it's the anesthesia or from him hitting his head in the accident but..." she said searching for the best way to prepare Sara for what she was about to say. She took a deep breath "He told me that his baby is going to die. And..." she nervously paused "Sara, he says it's his fault. We're not sure what he means, do you have any idea what he's talking about?"

"Actually I do," Sara replied. She looked down at her stomach, draping a protective arm around it "our baby is going to be just fine."

"Oh, thank God!" Nancy said clearly relieved. "We were starting to grow more concerned that it wasn't just some dream he was having. Of course we wanted to be sure that no one was in any real danger. They did search around the crash site trying to find a baby boy but... Well, now that you're here, maybe it will ease his mind and help him recover."

"I hope so" was all that Sara could say.

"Why don't you go on and be with your husband and I'll be right out here if you need anything."

"Thank you Nancy... for everything" Sara said attempting a smile but managing a brief grin.

She turned back to the door and put her hand on the silver handle and with a deep breath she pushed the lever down, opened the door slowly until she could see into the room.

CHAPTER TWENTY-SEVEN
Lifeless

Jacob was lying in a hospital bed slightly elevated, surrounded by monitors with various green lines or numbers all telling a different story about his current condition. Sara's eyes teared as the sight of Jacob lying in bed with tubes streaming off his body came into view.

When she neared his bedside a large bandage covered a shaved portion of his head, she gasped "Oh my God, Jacob!" She inched closer to his side. She could hardly recognize him. "What did you do?" She could feel her heart breaking for him.

On the monitor one of the numbers flashed an ominous red, setting off an alarm. A piercing single tone disturbed the silence of the room and startling Sara. She jumped back, a single hand immediately clasped her mouth to prevent her from adding to the

already obnoxious noise by screaming, her heart
pounded through her chest.

Within seconds a petite Asian looking woman with
olive colored skin entered the room with nurse's
scrubs on, went straight to the monitor emitting the
insufferable noise pushed some buttons and quickly
returned the room to its previously peaceful state.
She fiddled with a couple of the dozen or so wires
Jacob was connected to before she looked up at Sara,
sheepishly smiled and then quietly left the room.

It took Sara several moments to regain her
composure before she sat in an empty chair that was
placed opposite the monitors next to Jacob's bed. She
reached through the side rail on the bed and pulled
his hand into hers. "Oh Jacob, what did you do?
You're always so careful… I shouldn't have made
you leave, then maybe this wouldn't have happened.
I need you to be okay Jacob Michaels, I love you too
much to lose you."

She sat quietly trying not to allow her emotions
compromise her strength. She knew that Jacob
needed her to be strong for him. After nearly an hour
she couldn't take it anymore she had to let her
emotions out or she would explode. She gently got
up and laid his hand down ever so slightly. She
stepped out of his room, walked down the hall
searching for a secluded place.

"Can I help you with something Sara?" asked

Nancy.

"Actually yes, is there some place private I can make a call?"

"The family waiting room is just down the hall on the left. I'm fairly certain it's empty at this time of night. You could try there" Nancy said attempting a smile.

"Thank you" Sara said.

As soon as Sara entered the room and verified she was alone, she began to weep. The gravity of the Jacob's situation and the conflict between the two of them was too much to handle at the same time. She was heartbroken by it all and she didn't know what to do. She picked up her phone and dialed her mother-in-law, Betty.

The phone rang several times before she heard a click "Hello"

"Mom" was all Sara could say before she was overtaken by sobbing.

"Sara? Sara what's wrong dear?" Betty said.

"Mom, its Jacob. He was in an accident and he's in the hospital" she replied struggling to get all the words out.

"Oh my" Betty said "Is he…"

"He's not waking up and he's hooked up to all these machines," Sara interrupted. "I'm… well I," she paused to clear her throat "I knew you'd want to know."

"George, George wake up! Your son was in an accident" Sara could hear Betty trying to rouse Jacob's dad. "I swear you could sleep through a tornado!"

Sara told Betty everything she knew about Jacob's situation up to that point which wasn't much just that he'd miraculously survived his car accident. He did have some sort of head injury and was being heavily sedated but that was all she could report.

"We'll start making arrangements to come to Mountain Fork in the morning. It may take us a couple of days to get there.

"Well, I'll be talking to the doctors tomorrow. I'll let you know what they say and hopefully it will be good news" Sara said.

"That sounds good dear. One more thing. Talk to him, tell him how you feel. He might be asleep but he'll hear you" she said plainly.

"Okay, I will" was the only response Sara could muster. She hurried back to Jacob's room and quietly returned to the chair next to his bed. She sat for a while contemplating Betty's advice. Then she scooted the chair as close as she could, took his hand in hers once again and said "Jacob, I don't know if you can hear me or even if you want to talk to me but I have something I need to say to you. I love you more than I could ever explain and I want to be your wife. But when I saw our son's little heart beating I knew that

I loved him too. When I found out that he was going to have problems... I fell apart. I didn't handle it very well at all and I know how hard that was for you. The truth is I felt like my son had died. I know he didn't but it felt that way. I know this doesn't make much sense but Stacey helped me see that the reason it hurt so much was because *who* I thought our son would be died with his diagnosis but *our* son didn't die. All I know is that I love our son and I want to care for him no matter what we may have to face in the future. I'm sorry that you don't want to be a part of our son's life but that's okay. I'll let you go so you don't have to." By the time she'd finished her last sentence tears were quietly streaming down her cheeks.

A squeeze of her hand stopped her from continuing. His voice was raspy and weak but Jacob tried to speak, "Where am I?"

"Jacob?" she said quietly "can you hear me? You're in the hospital, you were in an accident but they said you'd be fine," she tried to explain.

"Alex?"

"Jacob, it's me Sara..." There was a sharpness, a fear in her voice that she couldn't quite place. *Had he forgotten her? What if he lost his memory forever?* She banished the thoughts and steadied herself for whatever was coming.

"Sara?"

"It's me, Sara. Your wife." She squeezed his hand reassuringly.

"Baby. I want to see the baby's face," he said groggily, his index finger lifting off the bed pointing in her direction.

She dug into her purse and pulled out the 4D picture of their son and held it up to him. "Here's the baby. He's fine!" she said softly. She waited for Jacob to respond but he just kept saying the name Alex. "Who's Alex?" She asked, her curiosity peaked by the name.

Jacob continued to speak but his words were mostly incoherent babbling. "He showed me..." his voice faded into several inaudible words before he uttered three more clear words "save my son."

"Jacob... Jacob, can you hear me?" she urged in her own desperation but he just continued his incoherent mumbling in his sleep. She listened intently hoping to hear anything intelligible. As each mumble came and went her optimism of him waking up diminished until she finally gave up any hope that he'd wake up, at least for now. The long drive and the early hour finally caught up to her and she drifted off to sleep still holding his hand.

CHAPTER TWENTY-EIGHT
Doctors

Her eyes were bleary when she woke. The sound of unfamiliar voices rousing her from sleep. They stood in white coats huddled at the edge of Jacob's bed, the tallest of them craning over his companions pointing at something on his clipboard. She shifted her weight audibly as she sat up, rubbing the sleep from her eyes.

The tallest man turned to meet her gaze, his eyes were deep and kind. He extended a hand towards her, "Mrs. Michaels?"

Wordlessly she nodded, taking his ruddy hand, shaking it very briefly before letting go. She shifted again so that her arm was touching Jacob's leg, feeling the void that his absence left.

"Good morning, I'm Dr. Andrews one of the resident neurologists on staff here," He spoke with the slightest accent, though she couldn't place it, "If you have a moment, I would like to go over your husband's situation with you and answer any questions you might have."

"I would like that very much." she replied. Her heart hurt for him again as she tried to prepare for what she would soon learn about Jacob's situation.

She could see his demeanor become more calculated and she could tell he was slightly uncomfortable with the pending conversation. "Your husband suffered a significant blow to the head in his car accident. The injury caused a hematoma in his brain."

"What does that mean exactly?"

"It means that he has some blood in his brain as well as some slight swelling. We've been monitoring him to see if we need to do a craniotomy but so far he's been really fortunate. His swelling hasn't increased, which is good." He offered her a small, reassuring smile. She was fairly certain he could sense her growing apprehension.

"How long will he be… um, asleep?" she hesitated, not totally sure she wanted the answer.

"That depends on him really. We could potentially be waiting anywhere from a few days to a few months. But we just simply don't know."

Her heart sank but she pressed him further, "Will he ever wake up?"

"In his case, I would say the likelihood is very high that he will…" he said looking over at him. "It would help if you talk to him and encourage him to wake up. Anything you can say that he might want to hear could help. Its good to reassure him that everything is going to be fine and how much you want him to wake up. It's has been shown to help in these types of cases." Sara just stood there trying to wrap her head around everything she'd just heard. "Did you have any other questions for me before I go?"

"No…" she said, pursing her lips and shaking her head. "No, thank you." They shook hands again, he nodded in understanding.

"Well, if you think of any other questions please let the nurses know and they'll page me," he said as he left.

Sara nodded. As the door closed both her hands reactively covered her face as tears welled up in her eyes. She cried silently for several minutes, then got down on her knees alongside Jacob's bed and began to pray, "Lord… it's me, Sara Michaels. I know it's been a while since we talked, I mean really talked but I need you. I'm lost and I don't know what to do anymore. I love him Lord and I need him to wake up. ."

She was torn. She wanted Jacob to wake up and recover but she was afraid of what he might say if he did. Would he be angry with her? Would he blame her for his accident? Or worse would he want to continue the conversation about their son? She was starting to feel a bit overwhelmed with all the questions whirling around in her mind.

She took out her phone and opened her Bible app. The screen came to life and opened randomly to Matthew 6:25. It was something similar to what she used to do as a girl, let the Bible fall open and read whatever page it happened to be on. She had believed that was one of the ways God talked to her. It might have been a stretch but out of curiosity she read the verse.

Therefore I say to you, do not worry about your life...

How can I not worry? My husband is... she didn't allow herself to finish the thought. She sat for a moment then leaned over and said "Jacob, please wake up. I need you here with me. I need you to wake up!" but he just laid there motionless except for the occasional involuntary twitch. She spent several hours talking to him; waiting, anticipating, looking for any sign that he was responding to her voice but there wasn't one.

Nancy came in to check his vital signs interrupting her failed attempt to rouse him. "Hi Sara, how are you holding up?"

She discretely wiped her face, then replied "I'm tired but I'm okay."

"I heard the doctors came and saw you. From

what I understand things are getting better." Her
words were a statement but it sounded more like a
question to Sara.

"Yeah, they said he's likely going to wake up. I've
been trying to talk to him hoping he'd respond
but..." Sara trailed off, putting her face into her
hands. She took a deep breath.

Trying to be encouraging Nancy said "Well, don't
give up... sometimes it takes time. Right now, there's
a lot of healing going on in his body." The nurse
placed a hand on her back, attempting to console her.
"I just wanted to add... I've been praying for you
and your family."

"I really appreciate that, Nancy." Sara gave her the
first genuine smile she had felt in days.

"Absolutely," she replied happily. "Why don't you
go get something to eat or call a friend. I'll be here to
take care of him."

She nodded in compliance. Maybe she was right,
maybe she just needed to get out of that tiny hospital
room. Still, she felt the weight of Jacob's presence in
the room. The little beeping heart monitor nagging at
her to stay but there was just nothing else she could
do. She wasn't completely out of the room before she
hit the speed dial button on her phone to call Stacey.

"Hey girl, what's up?" Stacey asked
enthusiastically as she answered the phone. Before
Sara could utter a word she burst into tears. "What's

wrong, Sara?"

Sara took a deep breath. "Stacey, Jacob's in the hospital, in ICU. He was in a car accident."

"Oh my God, Sara I'm so sorry. Are you okay? Do you want me to come to the hospital?"

"No, not right now" she replied quickly. "I'm sorry, I mean, this is something I have to do on my own. I just needed to hear a friendly voice."

"Well, you know I'm here for you."

"I know, that's why I called you" she replied softly. Sara told Stacey everything about Jacob's situation and about how he wasn't waking up.

"I understand but what's really bothering you?" Stacey asked. She always had a sixth sense about people especially if they were holding something back from her. She always said it was both a gift and a curse but today Sara was thankful for her insight.

"The thing is, I love Jacob and I want to wake up and recover so I can take care of him. But what if he wakes up he still doesn't want anything to do with our son?" she asked. "And now, with his accident and his recovery, I'll take care of him but how..."

Stacey interjected "I know this is hard Sweetie but you have always been stronger than you think you are. You can handle this too!"

"That's the thing, I don't know if I can handle the constant pressure of knowing he doesn't want our son but I can't just abandon him while he's recovering. I don't think I…"

"Now, hold on a minute! You have to have faith that God will provide a way. You don't need to figure this out right now, you just need to follow your heart. I promise you, everything will be fine" Stacey said firmly.

Sara allowed Stacey's confidence to settle her "Okay, you're right. I can handle this. I will handle this and anything else for that matter!"

"That's my girl! Now c'mon give me a little smile. You know I can hear if you're smiling or not so, just smile, right now, just smile. It'll make you feel better!" Stacey egged her on.

Finally, Sara smiled and immediately Stacey said, "Now don't you feel better?"

"How do you do that?"

"It's a gift. Now go be with your husband!"

"Okay, okay, I'll go. I'll call you later if I need you."

"I'll be here, you know I will. Love you!"

"Love you too!"

Sara hung up the phone and headed back into the hospital.

CHAPTER TWENTY-NINE
Change Of Heart

For several days she talked to Jacob as if he was already responding to her but he wasn't and it hadn't escaped her. His parents had come and gone also trying to make a connection. Sara had also called in some of Jacob's closest friends to try to get a reaction from him. Even Stacey had eventually made her way to the hospital to be there for Sara. Whenever Sara allowed her thoughts to wander they tended to take her to the most extreme possibilities; Jacob being crippled or never waking up. Her defense was to never allow herself to idle too long and having people around helped.

But at that moment it was just she and Jacob in the room. In desperation she picked up her phone and opened the Bible app again. It opened to Genesis 22 "Okay God tell me something, anything" she said as if God were standing in the room with her. The first scripture to jump off the page was verse fourteen: *And Abraham called the name of the place The Lord Will Provide* which took her back to the conversation she'd had with Stacey. "She said the same thing to me!" Sara was a little bewildered by the coincidence.

She went back and read the entire chapter about Abraham's faith. It became very clear what she had to do. She sat for a long time staring at the Bible on her phone before she finally said "Okay God, I have nothing left but to trust you, help me believe."

She leaned over Jacob's bed and got close to his ear and said "I love you with all my heart Jacob Michaels and I know you can hear me. I need you to come back to me right now. Do you hear me, right now. We can work this out but I need you here with me. Please, please come back to me." She was weeping silently into his shoulder when the pangs of nausea had reached her throat and she rushed off to the restroom in the corner of the room and expelled her stomach. She moved cautiously to the sink to wash her face and became fixated on herself in the mirror "I know you can do it Lord, help him wake up. I can't make him but you can."

Recounting her conversation with Stacey about having faith and having read about Abraham's incredible faith, she calmed her emotions before the queasiness overwhelmed her again. After a long day of battling her stomach, trying to talk to Jacob and praying, she was tired. She pulled the handle on the chair transforming it into a makeshift bed and closed her eyes. "It's up to you now," she said talking to God.

She could hear Jacob's voice whispering calling out to her from her sleep. She looked up to find Jacob's bed elevated to almost sitting and him whispering to a nurse just before she left the room. They were alone, she rubbed her eyes in disbelief. He turned to her and said "Hi Sara," still struggling to speak "I'm so glad you're here because I need to talk to you." He said holding his throat and wincing, each word he spoke clearly more painful than the last.

Sara's first thought was *Oh thank God, now I don't have to see him just lying there anymore.* She thought that once he woke up it would be a while before he could talk, so she was surprised to hear his voice. His hair was standing erect except for the bandage on his head, the bruises on his face had diminished but were still visible. He looked like hell and she instantly felt sorry for him. But she also knew she wasn't prepared for the conversation that she had anticipated he wanted to have "We can talk when you're feeling better." she insisted.

"No!" he said forcefully. As he spoke he jerked forward. Jacob had always been such an expressive speaker but the abrupt movement sent a searing pain through his chest. He winced again but continued, "this can't wait!"

"Okay" Sara said, a little taken by his unusually firm tone. She nodded for him to continue but because she'd presumed he wanted to continue their discussion about terminating her pregnancy, her anxiety to started to build.

"I met someone..." he started, she couldn't tell by his expression what he meant by that, his face still slightly swollen from the accident.

She immediately sat up in her chair, her attention now fully vested in what he wanted to say next. "His name is Alex and he and his dad showed me something amazing."

"Alex? I'm sorry did you say he?" Sara asked.

"Yes, he's a boy with Down syndrome. He's thirteen and... he showed me something remarkable!"

"Remarkable?" she said clearly confused "What's that?"

"Now, I know... that... it's okay if our son has Down syndrome, it's..." he struggled to get the words out. "It's nothing to be afraid of..." he coughed to clear his throat before continuing "...that it doesn't have to be a disability!" he said before letting his throat rest for a long pause.

Sara sat in shock of what she was hearing "It doesn't have to be?" she asked not sure what he was trying to say.

"No it doesn't, really, it's just a life challenge that he'll have to be overcome." He coughed "If we help him, he can be anyone or do anything he wants to." He paused "What I'm trying to say is… I know that our son can be who God made him to be!" he said it clearly struggling.

But Sara pressed "How did this Alex do all that? You've been in the hospital almost as long as you've been gone…" she said but her words went unnoticed by Jacob.

"I'll tell you all about it later it's a long story. What I need you to know now," he stopped, the emotions caught in his throat. His voice faded but he continued "…is that I love our son the way God made him. That, I want to be his dad and… and" his words broke off abruptly before he started to quietly sob. He pulled her hand up to his lips and gently kissed to bridge of her knuckles like he always loved to do.

Sara knew that Jacob rarely, if ever, cried. He was taught that men don't cry as a young boy and seeing him in such a vulnerable state stirred something inside of her. All she wanted was to be near him but her still pregnant belly prevented her from leaning over the bed for any length of time. They were forced to be content with holding hands in silence as they both wandered in thought.

When Jacob could finally speak again he said, "Will you please forgive me for not being a good husband and worse a good father to *our* son?"

Sara couldn't believe her eyes and her ears, "No, you aren't a bad anything. You couldn't have helped me no matter what you did. I had to work through it on my terms" she tried to explain but soon realized it was too much for him to deal with right then. She stopped, smiled at him and said "Actually, you need to forgive me for making you leave. You wouldn't be here right now if I hadn't..." she replied.

He put his finger up and shook it and his head 'no'. "It was the best thing that could've ever happened to me."

"How can you say that? Look where you are! Look what happened to you!"

"That doesn't matter. If you hadn't told me to leave then I would never met Alex. He helped me see who our son could be and helped me find something I didn't even know I lost."

"What's that?" Sara asked.

"My love for our son... True love."

"True love?"

"Yeah, the kind of love that's unconditional, the kind of love my son deserves no matter how he's born." Jacob said his voice fading in and out from the strain "And my faith in God's plan for him... and for us."

"God's plan," she said reflecting on her own revelation when she poured her heart out to Stacey and in her prayers "that's so strange Stacey said the same thing to me not long ago." She glanced out the window for a moment before looking back at Jacob "Are you sure you want to be the dad of boy who's different?"

He leaned toward her and looked directly into her eyes "I'm *absolutely* sure!" he replied resolved.

Not completely convinced she said "Now look, I can't take anymore of this craziness. If you have any doubts about this you need to tell me now because if you leave again…" she didn't finish her statement but knew he got her point.

Jacob replied firmly "I promise you that I'm in it for the long haul. I *want* to be our son's dad. I want to see him grow up to be the musician that I know he'll be."

"Musician? What makes you think he's going to be a musician?"

"Alex showed me in the newspaper who our son will be."

"Okay… Um, you believe him?" Sara asked concerned because Jacob seemed so convinced about what he was saying but what he was saying wasn't possible. No one can see the future and predict who someone will or won't be.

"Very much, yes I do!"

"I think I need to call Dr. Andrews in here and ask him take a look at you!" She said it calmly and for his sake in jest but she wasn't sure what to think. *He must've been hallucinating or had dreamed this up while he was in his coma* she thought.

"Just wait, I'll prove it to you when we meet Alex."

Sara stood up and bent down and gently kissed him "Okay... okay we'll make plans to visit Alex again but for now you need to rest," she said looking lovingly into his eyes. She was thrilled by his change of heart but she resolved to be cautiously optimistic. For now he needed her to be his wife and the woman he loved. She laid a hand on his cheek and said "I love you, Mr. Michaels!"

"I love you too, Mrs. Michaels!"

Sara sat back down, kissed his hand "Go ahead lay down. I'm not going anywhere, we can talk more later."

Within two weeks of him waking up at the hospital, Jacob had made a remarkable recovery and in that time, they'd shared many quiet, reflective moments. The bond they had and thought they'd lost was being knitted back together in a remote hospital in a small town.

Nancy lightly knocked on the hospital room door and motioned for Sara to come out. "I have to tell you Mrs. Michaels, I've never seen someone turn around so quickly from that kind of accident." Nancy said. "He must love you very much."

"He does and I love him *just* as much" she replied.

"Well, it looks like you all can start getting ready to head home, the doctor put in your discharge orders" Nancy said.

"Are you sure you don't want to keep him a while longer?" she asked playfully and they both laughed. But it wasn't long before they said their good-byes to the staff and were on the road headed home. The winding road symbolic of the dramatic twists and turns their lives had taken in those short weeks. They were going home thankful, holding hands and enjoying the beautiful countryside.

CHAPTER THIRTY
Going Back

It had been several months since Jacob and Sara
had returned home from the hospital. Jacob was had
nearly fully recovered from the four surgeries he'd
had to his broken leg and fractured skull. Over that
time he'd exhausted Sara with hours of tales of his
adventures with Alex and then retelling them as he
remembered more details about their time together.

Sara didn't know what to make of most of what he
told her. It sounded too much like a fantasy he'd
dreamed up but she wasn't sure how real any of it
really was. All she knew or cared about was that
Jacob was excited about being a dad and he didn't
care about their son's diagnosis anymore. Her
cautious optimism had given way to a hopeful
expectation of the future. He'd say repeatedly "When
our son is old enough, I'm going to get him a piano

and lessons or maybe a guitar… or both. And we'll have to take him to see some of Alex's concerts!"

As excited as he was at the prospect of being a dad, he was also consumed with seeing Alex again. "I really want to go back to Mountain Fork this weekend," he said giving Sara his best impression of a puppy dog look. "Pleaasee," he said stretching the vowels for effect.

"I don't know," she replied trying desperately not to give in to his boyish charm.

"Oh come on, please!" he said with a big smile, knowing she was about to cave. "You see? I'm fine!" he proclaimed then stood up leaving his aluminum cane at the desk and walked around to face her. He held his hand out prompting her to stand up from his executive chair he'd strategically placed across his desk when he first bought it. He put it there to give him a perfect view of her from his seat behind the desk. He gently pulled her in close, pressing his lips to hers hoping to seal the deal.

"Okay, we'll go but I'm driving…" she said hesitantly, "deal?"

"Deal!" he said excitedly before he whispered in her ear "I love you so much."

"I love you, too" she said with an almost motherly tone.

Returning to his office chair he pulled himself close to the desk. A quick Google search pulled up several theaters in Mountain Fork. Jacob clicked on images to try to identify the right one.

"It looks like there's only one symphony theater in the entire town..." he said. "Alex did tell me that it had the number 321 on the front of the building." He pulled up the image of the theater confirming his suspicion. Just above the main entrance prominently displayed were the numbers 321. "It's exactly how Alex described it" he said. *I bet the number is part of the address* Jacob thought as he opened the page from the image to find the address "The Theater at 321 Down Street, that's it!" he shouted excitedly. "And they have a show this weekend! Perfect! Do you want to go to the symphony with me?"

"Of course, I would love to go anywhere with you!" she said confidently.

"Well, you're the only one I want to go to a symphony with so... I guess it's a date!"

"Well then, we'll leave tomorrow morning, will that be satisfactory?" Sara said in the best comedic way she could muster, topped with a hint of sarcasm. She continued, "I'll get the bags ready. Will there be anything else?"

"Oh yes, would you tell my wife to be ready promptly by 9 am. I'd like to get to the theater before the prelude this time." he replied using his best rich British guy accent, attempting to match her wit but knowing she was far more talented than him at accents and impressions.

The next morning they pulled out of the driveway at 8:37 am, largely due to Jacob's constant prodding for Sara to speed up the process. For Jacob every minute of the drive felt like it hopelessly dragged on.

Sara started laughing as she watched her husband transform from a full grown man to a little boy, "This proves you can never get the little boy out of the man," she joked. "Pretty soon you'll be asking me if we're there yet!"

"Are we there yet?" Jacob replied smiling from ear to ear.

Although it had been months since they'd been on the winding road, it felt familiar. That and the fact that it was daytime allowed them to arrive in Mountain Fork more than thirty minutes earlier than she had before. Once again the blue triangle on her GPS guided her to her destination.

"We should go to the hotel first so I can introduce you to Alex" Jacob said.

"That sounds good. Maybe we could get checked in and freshen up a bit" she replied.

The air was cool but not cold like it had been the first time Jacob arrived at the hotel. He carefully exited the car and he and Sara walked hand-in-hand into the lobby. The same elderly man from his previous visit popped up from behind the counter.

"Can I help you folks?"

"Yes, we need a room for the weekend" Sara said.

"You bet-cha. I just need to see a driver's license and a major credit card" the innkeeper said.

"I should be in the computer already. I stayed here a few months back" Jacob said.

"Let me see, Michaels." He pecked the computer keys, his head tilted back slightly to look through the glasses at the end of his nose. "Oh, here you are. I knew I recognized you from before. As a matter of fact we held onto the things you left here from your last visit. I was wondering when you would come back to get them" the innkeeper said. He had a southern accent with a hint of someone who lived in the mountains all their lives.

"I'd forgotten all about those things to be honest with you. I kinda got sidetracked for awhile."

"Well, we heard that you'd been in a car accident when the police stopped by to check out your room. Not sure what they were looking for."

"Yeah..." he replied with his head down slightly embarrassed "I did have an accident and had to stay in the hospital for a while, sorry about that" Jacob said hoping he wouldn't ask any more questions about it.

"You were only here for a few hours before you came back down. You looked a little spaced out talking something about you needing to save your son or something like that. That might be why the cops searched your room, I'm guessin they couldn't tell if you were hyped up on drugs or if your boy was really in trouble… I don't know."

"You must've been out of it Jacob, exhausted or something…" Sara said.

"Well, you might want to ask yourself this question. Do you remember leaving the hotel that night?" the innkeeper said pointing out the obvious question.

"No but I did hit my head really hard so I just figured it was because of that" Jacob replied.

"Well, all I know is that when I tried to talk to you, you were here but… you weren't here, if you catch my drift" he said pointing to his head. "Anyway your room is ready and I put you in the same room you had before on the third floor, Mr. Michaels."

"Room 21?"

"Yep, that's the one. I guess you hitting your head didn't wipe out all your memories."

"I guess not," Jacob replied glancing down at Sara. He squeezed Sara's shoulders affectionately. "Hey, sir?"

"The name's Pete" he responded nonchalantly, without really looking up from his work.

"Pete. Let me ask you, when I was here before there was a boy who delivered newspapers to the rooms, Alex, is he here?"

"Not today, he's getting ready to perform at the Theater behind the hotel. He plays the piano. He's really quite good at it too!" Pete boasted.

"Is that the Theater with the 321 on it?"

"Yes Sir! The Theater at 321 Down Street! I named it that when I realized Alex was a magician on that piano of his."

"So, Alex *is* your son?" Jacob asked not sure if his previous conversation with Pete were real and not wanting to seem out of touch. Sara squeezed his hand to remind him not to be too forward with his questioning.

"He is. He's the best thing I never knew I always wanted."

"What do you mean?"

"I mean, I thought I wouldn't be a good enough dad for a boy like him. Really, I was just afraid. But he's the best thing that's ever happened to me... besides his mother.

"Forgive me for being so blunt but does Alex have Down syndrome? The reason I ask is because our son was diagnosed with it and well, I... uh."

"Think nothin of it. Yes, he's got Downs. But that's what makes what he can do on that piano even more spectacular. It's the reason I named that place 'The Theater at 321 Down Street'. You all want to go see his performance tonight?"

"Actually, when I was here last time Alex asked

me to come back and see him play and I promised him I would. It's part of the reason we came back."

"He must've liked you then Mr. Michaels. He doesn't invite people to watch him play unless you're really something special."

"Please, it's Jacob"

"Well then Jacob it is. And what's your name little lady?"

"Sara"

"Well, Jacob and Sara, I want to give you my front row tickets to watch Alex play tonight" Pete said excitedly.

"Awe that's sweet. But we're happy to pay for tickets to watch him" Sara replied.

"I insist you take my tickets. I want you to see how truly amazing Alex is at playing that piano from the *front* row. Now please make an old man happy and take my tickets." Pete said firmly.

They said it in unison looking at each other "We'd love to" and Jacob looking back at Pete continued "yes, we'd love to go. Thank you so much."

"Great, why don't you all head up to your room, get yourselves all gussied up and I get the tickets ready for you. Oh, and don't eat because dinner is covered with these tickets too. Just make sure you show up an hour before show time, okay."

"You got it my friend." Jacob said

Sara added "And Thank you so much Pete."

CHAPTER THIRTY-ONE

Master Musician

Sara stepped out of the bathroom and stood in front of Jacob. She was wearing a black sleeveless evening gown that flowed over her every curve down to her ankles. Her hair draped over the olive skin of her bare shoulders "You look absolutely stunning!" Jacob said.

"Well, I don't feel stunning. I feel like a blimp." She pouted, playfully sticking out her bottom lip.

"I'm your husband and I'm telling you, you're no blimp. You being pregnant just makes you even *sexier*. At least… to me it does and last time I checked my opinion is the one that matters, unless."

"Unless what?"

"Unless you've been shopping for a younger, newer model. After all, I've been in a wreck." Jacob teased. He tapped the scar from his head injury which was still noticeable to anyone who knew what to look for. "Damaged goods"

She walked toward him contemplatively. With her index finger over her lips she tapped; her eyes looking skyward and slightly to the right. "Nah, then I would have to start all over training him. Too much work for me" she winked breaking into a smile then sliding her arms under his to enjoy his warm embrace.

"I'm telling you. You look beautiful" Jacob whispered.

"Okay" she replied biting her lip, a small blush coloring her cheeks. "I'll take your word for it."

"Are you ready to go?"

"Yes I am handsome," Sara said.

Jacob opened the door to usher her out. When they returned to the lobby Pete was waiting for them with tickets in hand. "Follow me please" he came out from behind the reception counter by lifting a hinged section and then opened a door that led them down a service hallway through another door and into the first floor hall. He turned and walked to the end as they both followed him around the corner to the service elevator.

"That's the elevator that Alex took me down." Jacob whispered to Sara. They all climbed on and Pete pushed the button sending the elevator down to the basement. When they stepped off Jacob said

"This is the one. We go down here and it turns to the right. Then we go all the way down the hallway to the double doors."

As Jacob predicted they turned right at the end of the entry way but it wasn't the same. "When I was here before this place was dark and creepy. I don't understand." When they reached the end of the hallway, there in front of them was a set of identical wooden doors. "Where are the faces?" Jacob asked unintentionally out loud.

"Faces?" Pete asked.

"I've seen these doors before and there were faces of children carved into them and now they're gone. What happened to them?"

"I don't know anything about any faces. These are how these doors have always looked ever since we installed them about seven years ago or so. Well, come to think of it the doors that were here before had those theater masks on them, you know one is happy and one is sad."

"It wasn't those. Maybe it wasn't the same doors" Jacob replied confused.

Sara noticed the distressed look on Jacob's face and asked "Are you okay?"

"I'm fine, I'm just a little mixed up I guess."

"It'll be okay" she assured him, patting him affectionately on his arm.

Pete pushed open the doors but instead of entering

the theater they walked into a fully operational restaurant. Pete leaned over to the hostess and whispered to her before he turned back to them and said "You kids enjoy yourselves tonight and don't worry about anything it's all been taken care of, okay?"

"We will Pete, again thank you so much. We really appreciate it." Sara said.

Pete nodded before he disappeared back into the hallway. "Are you ready?" the hostess asked. Sara tugged on Jacob's arm and they followed her to a quite table in the back.

As soon as they were alone Sara asked "Baby, are you sure you're okay?"

Jacob shook his head to dismiss all his questions "Yeah babe, I'm fine. I just don't understand… I thought…" he shook his head casting out all his confusion and doubt. "What matters is I'm here with you and our son." He lifted her hand and gently kissed it, smiled and said "I can't wait to see the show."

"I can't wait either." She smiled at him.

They laughed and talked as they ate. Then Sara said rubbing her belly "We can't just keep calling this boy 'our son'. We need to give him a name… any thoughts?" she asked pointedly.

Jacob was stumped, he sat for a moment and contemplated her question. "Um, I haven't had a chance to think about it honestly." Out of the corner of his eye Jacob could see the hostess heading toward their table leading with a bright smile.

She leaned gently toward them "I'm sorry folks" she said sensing she'd interrupted an important conversation "but the show will be starting soon. Please allow me to show you to your seats." She stepped back to allow them to get up from their table and gestured for them to follow.

As requested they followed her through some more double doors and entered the theater. It was exactly how Jacob remembered it, every detail from the carpet to the seats, adding to his confusion. As he looked up he saw the pearl white grand piano placed in the center of the stage.

"Wow," Sara said "this is beautiful."

They sat in the seats at the center of the theater on the front row and watched as the building filled with people to its capacity. "Would you look at that, all these people are here to see Alex play. That's amazing!" Jacob said.

"I know. Honestly I wouldn't have believed it, if I wasn't seeing it for myself" Sara added.

"I'm telling you, Alex is truly amazing" Jacob said adamantly.

Moments later the lights dimmed, the spotlight came on and Alex walked to the center of the stage. He was dressed in a black tuxedo with a long tail. He stood in front of the bench for a moment his black jacket contrasting against the piano. Then like a professional he flipped the tail of his tux just before sitting squarely in the center of the bench. He raised his hands and placed them on the keys.

The punchy sounds of Beethoven's Sonata Hammerklavier soon filled the room. The audience watched in pure amazement as Alex, a boy many in the world had said wasn't capable of normal because he has Down syndrome, performed the piece with the skill of the composer himself. The audience popped to their feet and into a roaring applause. Jacob and Sara came out of their seats with the fervor of parents applauding their own son.

As the crowd settled, the music softened and they watched intently as Alex worked up and down the keys of the piano. Jacob glanced over toward Sara who was so immersed in the experience of watching the concentration in Alex's eyes and the passion in his face her mouth hung open. Jacob gently reached over putting one finger below her chin and lightly lifted.

She barely gave him a glance as she closed her mouth and gave her attention completely to his performance. Jacob returned his attention to Alex as well. Soon, the final notes echoed across the room as it erupted into cheers and applause. Alex stood to take a bow when he saw Jacob on the front row. A smile burst onto his face and he hurried to the edge of the stage and jumped down right in front of Jacob. The audience gasped and the spotlight struggled to keep up. "You came just like you promised!" Alex exclaimed as he reached out to hug Jacob.

Jacob reveled in his embrace "Hi Alex, I'm so glad to see you."

"Did you see me play?" Alex asked as he looked up at Jacob.

"I did. And you were amazing but don't you need to finish?" Jacob asked.

"Oh yeah" Alex said laughing as if it were no big deal. "Come on" Alex said tugging on Jacob's hand.

"No, this is your concert. You don't need me up there" Jacob said.

"I don't *need* you but I want you to be there with me. I have a surprise for you."

Not wanting to cause any more of a scene than was already being caused Jacob complied. "Okay, buddy let's go."

Alex led Jacob up to the stage and stopped to face the crowd. "Stay here" Alex told Jacob as he quickly went to retrieve a microphone. He used his finger to tap it before saying "Good evening everyone, my name is Alex and this is my buddy Jacob. That means we're friends. He was in a very bad accident and I talked to him and played music for him. He promised to come see me play and he did and I'm very happy about that. Please say hi to Jacob everybody."

"Hi Jacob" the audience called out.

"Here, tell them why we're buddies" Alex said holding the microphone out to Jacob.

Jacob shook his head no but the happiness in Alex's eyes captivated him and he reached out for the microphone before he realized what he was doing. He hesitated for what felt like an eternity, the anticipation from the audience was thick enough that Jacob could feel its weight. He finally raised the mic to his mouth "Uh, um... Good evening everyone, my name is Jacob Michaels. Um, please forgive me, I'm... I'm a bit nervous."

"You'll be okay buddy" Alex said smiling.

"Why are me and Alex buddies? Well, the simple answer is because he saved me from myself and changed my life. You see... um, my wife and I are having a son" the audience clapped but Jacob held up his hand in protest. "He'll be born with Down syndrome and... at first... um," Jacob's throat thickened "at first, I didn't want my son because he wasn't the son that I expected." Tears welled up in his eyes before streaming down his face as he recalled the mirror exploding on the very stage where he now stood. "My son was supposed to be like me. He would look like me or his mom and..." Jacob paused to see Sara crying. He looked directly at her and continued "I thought my son had to be what I thought was normal in order for me to be happy. I also thought that I couldn't be... I mean, that I wasn't capable of being the dad of an innocent little boy, whose only problem in the world was that he'd be born different" Jacob covered his eyes but he couldn't hold back his emotions.

The audience unsure of what to do started clapping. Jacob tried to continue "I, uh" but another wave of emotions grabbed hold oh him. Jacob took several deep breaths to regain his composure "but then... then I met Alex. And *he* is truly amazing."

The audience clapped "I appreciate you clapping for him, he certainly deserves it. He has a gift that is so obvious, his ability to play that piano is awe inspiring. But that's not the gift I'm talking about. He has the gift of innocence. He can sense someone else's pain and he has more compassion in the fingers that play that piano than most of us have in our entire existence."

He turned to Sara and said "I'm not even sure how much of what Alex and I did together was real but... on this very same stage he... he showed me who my son could be. And even if my son doesn't become a super star or a master musician. If... if he's anything like the Alex that I've come to know that's good enough for me" Jacob said weeping.

Alex turned to Jacob with a teary smile on his face

and gave him a bear hug "I love you buddy."

"I love you too, Alex" Jacob said, then turned to the audience and said "that's why we're buddies" he said. His attention turned to Sara who was shedding tears but these weren't saddened tears but they were tears of joy. That was the moment that Sara realized why Jacob was so desperate to come back to see Alex.

Alex reclaimed the mic and said "I'd like to play one more piece for you tonight that I wrote for my buddy, Jacob." Alex suddenly stood up straight, did a military style about face and walked toward the piano. Alex sat back down and began to play. Jacob hurried back to his seat and to Sara. The music that filled the room pulled Jacob back to the last time he and Alex were on that same stage. *That's the music he played before!* But *wasn't that from a dream?* he thought confused. Sara glanced at him and then took a second look as he rubbed some tears from his eyes. She reached out and interlocked her fingers with his and then leaned her head down onto his shoulder.

As Alex completed his own song the crowd gave him a standing ovation and shouted for encore after encore until Pete finally came out from backstage and announced. "We want to thank you all for coming. Please feel free to come back tomorrow night if you'd like to see Alex play again. God bless and good night."

As the crowd stood clapping, Pete motioned for Jacob and Sara to come up and then ushered them backstage. "I told you he was amazing, didn't I?"

"You did and he was!" Sara replied because Jacob was still choked up. His eyes were red and puffy from all his recent blubbering so he nodded in agreement.

"I wanted you to see him perform before I told you something that may clear up some of your confusion Jacob."

"Oh yeah, what's that?" Jacob asked hesitantly.

"Alex volunteers at the hospital and he insisted on visiting you every day you were there. That is until Sara showed up. He didn't want you to be alone. He told you stories, talked to you like the doctor's suggested and he even played some of his music for you. He recorded it on one of those iPad things. I don't know how but you made quite an impact on him while you were there."

"I made an impact on him!? Pete, I think you have it backwards. He made me see my son. My real son for who he is... a gift from God to me, to Sara... to the world. I don't care if it was a dream or a vision or what is was. Meeting your son changed my life" he said passionately.

"Well, thank you Jacob. You saying that means a lot to me" Pete said somberly.

Alex hurried toward them "Jacob, Buddy!" Alex

shouted as he came out of his dressing room. He was transformed back to the boy he'd met when he first came to the hotel. He wore a maroon colored, long sleeve shirt un-tucked and blue jeans with red shoes.

"Alex you are truly, truly amazing" Jacob said.

"Thank you! I like playing the piano for people, especially my friends, like you buddy!" Alex's innocence was on display.

Jacob stepped forward, lightly pulling Sara toward Alex introducing them to each other. Sara was a little nervous at first, carefully observing the child in front of her. Alex smiled warmly at her. He quickly held out his hand for her to shake. When she took too long, he took hold of her hand placed it into his open hand to show her how a handshake was properly done. He smiled at her and she could feel his warmth.

"You're so silly! Nice to meet you, Mrs. Michaels."

"Nice to meet you too Alex, you can call me Sara if you'd like and thank you for looking after Jacob for me. I really do appreciate that" Sara said emphatically.

He was enthusiastic at her words. He hugged her softly, hyper aware of her protruding stomach. "Thank you Sara and you're welcome. He's my Buddy."

"Yes, I am" Jacob said. Right then, in the middle of their reunion a smile exploded onto Jacob's face as he

227

announced "I have it!"

"Have what?" Sara asked.

"You asked me a question at dinner. You remember what it was?"

"About our son's name?"

"That's the one!" he paused for effect "John Alex Michaels"

"John Alex Michaels... hmm, John Michaels" Sara said several times. "That rolls off the tongue perfectly. And it feels right to me..." Sara said excitedly before suddenly realizing her present company "oh, with your permission of course" she said looking at Pete.

"It would mean a lot to me, since your son changed my life." Jacob said.

"He changed mine too" Pete replied candidly. "Of course I don't mind. Who am I to stand in the way of a perfect name?"

"John Alex Michaels it is!" Jacob announced.

Jacob and Sara stayed the weekend visiting with Pete and Alex. Alex's story gave them a fresh new hope and an understanding of the future possibilities for their son. And so, there at a hotel in the small town of Mountain Fork, John Michaels journey began!

The End!

CHAPTER THIRTY-TWO

In Their Own Words

Allow me to preface these words by saying that our son, John-Michael, is a blessing to our family and the events of his birth were from a position of fear and ignorance.

We discovered that John-Michael had Down syndrome the day he was born which was confirmed two weeks later by testing. It was late November of 2012 early in the morning when my wife started having intense contractions. We rushed off to our alternative birthing center (our last three kids were born there and not a hospital) where in less than two hours our son entered the world.

In the months leading up to that day we were seeing a specialist twice a month to perform an ultrasound. She suspected John-Michael may have Downs but we'd refused the amniocentesis and we refused to believe it was possible.

As people of faith, we prayed daily that our son would be born healthy and whole and the day he was born sent us on our own path to self-discovery. Although this book is fiction, the emotions, the fear and the pain are all the same things we experienced. You see, when John-Michael was born he had so much extra skin, it looked like the rolls of an elderly person. And to be truthful it shocked us so badly we weren't sure how to react. We knew we were supposed to be happy but it felt more like we'd slipped through a wormhole and were experiencing someone else's life. This wasn't supposed to happen to us, we are believers.

Needless to say, we when through a bizarre time of grieving, a depressed state where we didn't know what to do and didn't want to tell anyone. When we did finally tell a close friend of ours, she asked another friend who had also got the same diagnosis prenatally, to call my wife, Marianne. She told us how she experienced the exact same emotions and also explained that she related it to the grief we experience when a loved one passes away. I know it's crazy, right?

Not long after that we were introduced to Lisa and Eric and their son Landon who at the time was just three years old. We spent the afternoon with them one Sunday and got a sneak a peek into the future of raising a son with Down syndrome. I have to tell you, it was the best thing that could've happened. The fear of the unknown had suffered a major blow that day and we were on the road back to happiness.

I truly believe the message portrayed in this book, that our kids may have challenges, especially all kids with Down syndrome and Autism and other developmental delays. They may have more than others but does that make them weak? Or does it make them stronger? In my experience the more challenges any person overcomes the stronger they become but in the eyes of a world who determines what is and what isn't normal it makes them weak.

I would propose to you that if you're a parent of a child diagnosed with Down syndrome or for that matter any developmental delay, find someone else who has already walked the road you're about to travel down and see what your future holds. I honestly believe that it'll change your whole outlook and you'll likely make a friend.

And if you need someone to connect with please email me at: info@johnmichaelsjourney.com

It had a been an extremely easy pregnancy...no morning sickness, no worries. This was my second child and we were delivering in the same hospital, so I knew what to do, or so I thought.

231

321 DOWN STREET

I decided not to do the genetic testing because it would not change my decision to have my child and I thought knowing there was a problem would cause undo stress on my pregnancy.

My second son decided to come a month early, just like my first.

Upon delivering my son, I knew instantly that something was not right. Not by the nursing staff or by my husband who kept telling me how beautiful our son was. It was there in my son's eyes. The second I made eye contact, I knew that something was different.

Despite my concerns, everyone assured me I had a healthy baby boy and so we proceeded to make phone calls to all our family and friends to announce the birth of our second child. Then, four hours later, our world came to a screeching halt.

Our pediatrician came into our hospital room and from his body language we could tell he was upset and uncomfortable. He couldn't make eye contact and words were escaping him. Then he said, "Your son appears to have many of the features of a child with down syndrome". Boom! At that instant...what should have been a joyous occasion turned into a

painful reality. The future we had planned for and
the dreams we had hoped for, just died. I will be
honest and say it became hard to look at my son and
be happy. I was scared. What did this mean? What
is down syndrome? What type of brother will he
be? Will people accept him? Can I do this? Why
me?

No one knew how to talk to us or how to treat us.
It was like we had a disease. So much so, we were
moved from our hospital room to another room in
the corner, away from everyone else. We were
already being shunned!

In addition to feeling lost, the nursing staff and
neonatologist were cold and heartless. I vividly
remember a nurse asking me why I didn't do the
genetic testing, clearly implying that I should have
terminated the pregnancy. Within hours of my son's
birth, I was already being asked to justify his right to
live because he was not typical. Another nurse told
us that my husband had been labeled the angry
father and we were being avoided. Maybe that was
why my post pregnancy needs were neglected. I
waited almost 24 hours to get the essentials that
mothers of healthy newborns get almost
instantaneously. And the neonatologist told me I
needed to accept the diagnosis and start embracing

my son.

We did have a handful of nurses that felt it was necessary to try to make us feel better by giving us the false hope that our son could be typical. They told us there was a possibility that he just showed the features of down syndrome, yet he could outgrow them. Of course, we clung to these hopes and prayed that our son would be typical and healthy. These ended up being false hopes that should have never been instilled in a family that needed truths to start planning for the uncertain future that lied ahead.

We also learned that children with down syndrome have a 50% chance of having a heart defect, so a cardiologist was being called to do an echocardiogram on our son's heart. Although my son was delivered on a Friday, we would wait until Sunday to have the echocardiogram and meet with the cardiologist. In the meantime, nurses listened to our son's heart and told us they were hearing no signs of leaks or holes, so the probability of him having a heart defect was very slim. What a relief to parents that just had their world turned upside down. But then, on Sunday, the second set of heartbreaking news came. Our son did have a heart defect that would require open heart surgery. It ends up the larger the hole in the heart, the less likely doctors and nurses are able to detect it without an echocardiogram.

The next 6 months were crazy. Friends, family and colleagues accepted our news in different ways. I remember people not knowing what to say or do. My husband's employer even questioned if my husband would be able to do his job which filled our world with additional worries. Friends reached out, yet I didn't want to talk to them in fear that I would cry. No matter what, I always felt like I had to be strong for everyone else. I felt as though I had to make them feel comfortable with my son's diagnosis, even though deep down, I was still struggling with the diagnosis myself.

In the middle of all the chaos came one nurse that will forever hold a place in my heart. She had come to our room to do the newborn hearing screening and she could see the pain and hurt we were feeling. Her name was Tiffany and she asked if she could say a prayer for our beautiful son. She was the only person, besides family, that said our son was a gift and true blessing. And yes, indeed, Tiffany was correct. Despite all the grieving and all the uncertainty, my son is indeed a blessing that teaches me daily the meaning of true love, honesty, strength, determination and living life to the fullest.

321 DOWN STREET

Our family of four is now a beautiful family three...myself and my two boys. We are a strong and determined trio that are thankful for each other and every day we have together. We love deeply, live in the moment, find pleasure in life's little things and support each other's unique hopes and dreams. This is our journey and we wouldn't change a thing.

When our son, Blakeley, was born in 1998 with Down syndrome, I was plunged into a very dark place. More than anything, I wanted Down syndrome GONE from my child, so that he could be the son that I had imagined. Then one night, as a sat watching him sleep, I was filled with an overwhelming sense that Blakeley was EXACTLY as he was meant to be. That he was perfect in every way and that everything was going to be fine. That feeling has not changed from that day to this and he is the joy and delight of our family. I can only name that experience as the grace of God. A gift not looked for or earned, but one that changed by life utterly.

Made in the USA
San Bernardino, CA
23 February 2016